We Interrupt This Broadcast

UPDATED SECOND EDITION

The Events That Stopped Our Lives... from the Hindenburg Explosion to the Death of John F. Kennedy Jr.

Joe Garner

SOURCEBOOKS, INC.®
NAPERVILLE, ILLINOIS

Copyright © 2000 by Joe Garner
Cover Copyright © 2000 by Sourcebooks, Inc.
Foreword Copyright © 2000 by Walter Cronkite
Cover Design by Eric O'Malley and Rebecca Pasko, Sourcebooks, Inc.
Book Design by Kirsten Hansen and Rebecca Pasko, Sourcebooks, Inc.

Front cover photos, left to right: Archive Photos; Archive Photos; Popperfoto/Archive Photos; Corbis
Foreword photo (Walter Cronkite): CBS, Inc., Steve Friedman
Author photos on page 169: Joe Garner by Sandy Speer; Bill Kurtis by Bridget Rowley
Back cover photos, left to right: Archive Photos; Reuters/Archive Photos; Corbis

Audio Credits, Photo Credits, and Copyrights at back

All rights reserved. No part of this book may be reproduced in any form or by any electronic or mechanical means including information storage and retrieval systems—except in the case of brief quotations embodied in critical articles or reviews—without permission in writing from its publisher, Sourcebooks, Inc.

Published by Sourcebooks
P.O. Box 4410
Naperville, Illinois 60567-4410
(630) 961-3900
Fax (630) 961-2168

Library of Congress Cataloging-in-Publication Data
Garner, Joe.
    We interrupt this broadcast: The events that stopped our lives—from the Hindenburg Explosion to the death of John F. Kennedy Jr. / Joe Garner.—2nd. [revised and updated] ed.
        p.   cm.
    ISBN 1-57071-535-1   (alk. paper)
    1. Television broadcasting of news. 2. Radio journalism. 3. Disasters—Press coverage. I. Title.
    PN4784.T4G36   2000
    070.1'95—dc21   00-022746

Printed and bound in Canada

TR   10 9 8 7 6 5 4 3 2 1

This book is dedicated to my Mom and Dad, Jim and Betty Garner,
for teaching me to dream. And to my wife Colleen,
my son James (J.B.), and my daughter Jillian,
for their love and support that
allows me to keep dreaming.

Table of *Contents*

Foreword
by Walter Cronkite

We are living through a period in history when journalism again faces great responsibilities and unexpected challenges.

This generation of journalists is faced with the heavy responsibility of recording as faithfully and honestly as is humanly possible the vast political and economic reorganization of the postwar era. That would be a demanding task even if our own profession was entirely stable and we could count on pursuing our craft with the wisdom assembled through past experience.

But that, alas, is not the case. Television has changed the face of journalism. In a time when, using the magic tube, political leaders can go over the heads of their own parties, when heads of state soar over national boundaries to address the people of other countries, the journalist's job takes on a new dimension. In broadcasting, there is need for instant analysis and the provisions of background information so that the people shall not be misled by skillful demagogues with these new means of persuasion at their command.

Such is also the need when the big stories break, and I have covered more than a few of them. When the events that change the world occur, we journalists must step up with all the instant thoughtfulness and knowledge we can muster in the face of triumph or tragedy.

It is an interesting thing about newspeople. We are much like doctors, nurses, firemen, and police. In the midst of tremendous events, our professional drive takes over and dominates our emotions. We move almost like automatons to get the job done. The time for an emotional reaction must wait. Even so, we are, at the same time, very human. When something changes your life, it also changes ours.

It is an interesting thing about newspeople. . . . The time for an emotional reaction must wait. Even so, we are, at the same time, very human.

I covered all the moon shots, but the pinnacle of all of them, and of my quarter century covering them, was seeing Neil Armstrong set foot on the surface of the moon. I believe that of all our achievements in the twentieth century, this is the one that students will read about in history books hundreds of years from now.

My reaction to the landing reflected that belief—it was goose pimples on goose pimples. When the moment came for Neil to step out of the *Eagle*, I was speechless.

"Oh boy! Whew! Boy!" I said, profundity to be recorded for all the ages. I had just as long as NASA to prepare for that moment, and yet, these were my words. They reflected my joy, awe, and admiration for those remarkable astronauts and for the daring and courageous spirit of humankind.

As is the nature of many events which warrant interrupting broadcasts, I also was there to report on the terrible tragedies.

Our flash reporting the shots fired at President John F. Kennedy's motorcade was heard over the "CBS News Bulletin" slide and interrupted the soap opera *As the World Turns*.

For the first hour, I reported sketchy details to a nation in shock. Then came the report from Eddie Barker, news chief of our Dallas affiliate, and Bob Pierpoint, our White House correspondent. They had learned the President was dead.

We were still debating in New York whether we should put such a portentous but unofficial bulletin on the air when, within minutes, the hospital issued a bulletin confirming the news. It fell to me to make the announcement.

My emotions were doing fine until it was necessary to pronounce the words: "From Dallas, Texas, the flash—apparently official. President Kennedy died at 1 p.m. central standard time—a half hour ago…"

The words stuck in my throat. A sob wanted to replace them. A gulp or two quashed the sob, which metamorphosed into tears forming in the corners of my eyes. I fought back the emotion and regained my professionalism, but it would be a few seconds before I could continue: "Vice President Johnson has left the hospital in Dallas, but we do not know to where he has proceeded. Presumably, he will be taking the oath of office shortly, and become the thirty-sixth President of the United States."

The potential of journalism today is greater than it has ever been. Today, news people in general are far better educated than ever, many holding advanced degrees. With strong academic backgrounds, they have been far more aggressive in covering politics, business, and the social movements of our time.

At the same time, this potential is often nullified by the problems facing the journalistic

> *Press freedom is essential to our democracy, but the press also must not abuse this license. We must be careful with our power.*

profession, problems which impact the core of our democratic society. Today's journalists face continual pressures from corporate ownerships and stockholders to dramatically increase profits. This requirement often means less reporters, writers, and editors covering more territory. It can also push good journalists in the direction of the sensational, the *entertainment* aspects of the news. The end result is a press lacking a sense of public service, which is the vital, fundamental component the press contributes to the nation's welfare.

Press freedom is essential to our democracy, but the press also must not abuse this license. We must be careful with our power. We must avoid, when possible, publicity circuses that make the right of a fair trial a right difficult to uphold. We must avoid unwarranted intrusions upon people's privacy. Liberty and, no less, one's reputation in the community are terribly precious things, and they must not be dealt with lightly or endangered by capricious claims of special privilege.

Above all else, however, the press itself must unwaveringly guard the First Amendment guarantees of a free press. The free press, after all, is the central nervous system of a democratic society. No true democracy, as we understand the term, can exist without it. The press may be irresponsible at times, obstreperous, arrogant, even cruel when innocent individuals are caught in the riptide of damaging publicity. But a free, unintimidated, and unregulated press is democracy's early-warning system against both the dangers of democracy's own excesses and the approach of tyranny. And inevitably, one of the first signs of tyranny's approach is its heavy footstep on the threshold of press freedom.

The preservation of our liberties depends on an enlightened citizenry. Those who get most of their news from television probably are not getting enough information to intelligently exercise their voting franchise in a democratic system. As Thomas Jefferson said, the nation that expects to be ignorant and free expects what never can and never will be. We can bring that up-to-date and amplify it a bit: the nation whose population depends on the explosively compressed headline service of television news can expect to be exploited by the demagogues and dictators who prey upon the semi-informed.

The secret of our past success as a nation may be traced to the fact that we have been a free people, free to discuss ideas and alternatives, free to teach and learn, free to report and hear, free to challenge the most venerable institutions without fear of reprisal. The First Amendment, with its guarantees of free speech and a free press, has been at the heart of the American success story. It must be guarded zealously if we are to gird for the challenges of the new century ahead.

Introduction
by Joe Garner

My passion for radio and television has been lifelong. With the exception of an occasional time-out for projects like this book, I've been fortunate to make a career of it.

As early as five or six years of age, I would sit in front of the TV at my homemade "set" which consisted of a couple of empty toilet tissue rollers, with a string attached for a microphone, Scotch-taped to the top of a TV tray. My mother was a great microphone maker. I sat there imagining that I was the host of the game show, a panelist on a talk show, then the anchor of the afternoon news. "Welcome ladies and gentleman" and "we'll be back in a moment" were as much part of my developing vocabulary as "What's for dinner?"

I recall how thrilled I was a few years later when the mailman finally delivered the set of records I'd ordered through a television offer, titled *The Golden Days of Radio*, presented by the Longines Symphonette Society. The five-record set contained excerpts of old-time radio serials that I couldn't wait to hear, like *Burns and Allen*, *Fibber McGee and Molly*, and *The Shadow*. The special bonus record contained the original broadcast of *War of the Worlds*. I still have those records.

But television and radio made sure that growing up in a small midwestern college town was no protection from the turbulence of the 1960s. The Vietnam War, assassinations, and the violence of the civil rights struggle came into our home just as it did into homes in much larger cities all across the country. I became keenly aware at an early age of another broadcast term, one that brought our household to silence as we waited to hear the news that followed. If you think about it, few other phrases in our language can cause the same split-second, heart-stopping anxiety as "We interrupt this broadcast."

As we approach a new millennium, I thought it important to assemble a compilation of these famous and infamous moments of this century, beginning at the dawn of electronic media, that stopped us in our tracks. They are the moments that have come to define our lives. They are the sudden catastrophes, the horrific beginnings and sometimes victorious ends to war. They are the senseless acts of terrorism, cold-blooded assassinations, and triumphant achievements of the human spirit.

While paging through a sample of this book, a veteran evening news anchorman for a major television network was overheard to say sarcastically, "I've interrupted a few broadcasts in my day, but that was back when they meant something." Today, the emergence of the twenty-four-hour cable news networks, the fierce competition among broadcasters, and the technology to beam it live from anyplace at anytime, has created an insatiable appetite for news. The results include never-ending debates over what constitutes a real news event, and the birth of a new broadcast term: "tabloid television."

Although it has become a popular pastime to criticize the media, this book is a tribute of sorts to radio and television and its journalists. Often, as you will read and hear, these events caught them as much by surprise as they did us. Yet, under stressful, sometimes dangerous circumstances, they skillfully performed their task with professionalism and compassion.

The events contained in this book were selected because they have stood the test of time. The sounds and images have become part of our very memories. We remember where we were when they happened and how we felt when we first heard the news. Each event is presented as it occurred, allowing you to be in the moment again, or perhaps for the very first time. Prepare to relive the events that have changed our outlook on the world forever.

"We Interrupt This Broadcast for a Special Bulletin..."

The Hindenburg *Explodes*

May 6
1937

Left to right:
The *Hindenburg* over
New York City •
The lounge aboard
the *Hindenburg* •
The *Hindenburg*

The *Hindenburg* was a spectacle of zeppelin design, described as a "floating palace" nearly as large and as grand as the *Titanic*—and as doomed. It was to be the first of a fleet of luxury lighter-than-air ships ushering in a new era of Trans-Atlantic zeppelin travel. Its lavish accommodations for fifty passengers and a crew of thirty included a fine dining room and an elegant lounge. Brochures boasted of reaching America from Germany in an astonishingly short two days at a price of $400. American Airlines even provided connection service to the *Hindenburg*.

At a cost of more than $5 million, the *Hindenburg* was the largest airship of its kind, measuring 804 feet in length. Its gigantic framework measured ten stories high, with catwalks and support beams traveling from nose to rear. Propelling the ship were four twelve hundred horse-powered Mercedes Benz engines, supplied with enough fuel to travel eleven thousand miles and permitting a top speed of eighty-four miles per hour.

But the Deutsche Zeppelin-Reederei Company, operators of the *Hindenburg*, was struggling financially, soliciting much of the funds for the construction of the airship from the Nazi party. In return, the airship, displaying swastikas on its fins, flew as a symbol for the power of Hitler's Third Reich. The United States, the only source for helium in the world, was growing suspicious of the potential military uses of the great zeppelins, and priced the amount of gas the *Hindenburg* would need at $600,000. In frustration, the Germans filled the *Hindenburg* with seven million cubic feet of highly volatile hydrogen gas instead of the fireproof helium.

Having successfully made ten round-trips between Germany and the United States in its one-year history, the landing of the *Hindenburg* was a wondrous sight. On May 6, 1937, storms

The Hindenburg was featured in German propaganda films bearing the Nazi swastika.

delayed its arrival from Frankfurt, Germany, into Lakehurst, New Jersey, by ten hours. The airship cautiously hovered over the mooring mast waiting out the treacherous weather conditions before attempting to land.

It was approximately 7 p.m. when the landing lines were dropped to the crew below and the *Hindenburg* was carefully guided in. With the mooring only minutes from completion, Herb Morrison, a thirty-one-year-old reporter from Chicago radio station WLS, was on the ground recording the landing. But the landing suddenly went terribly awry, as smoke and flames burst from the rear section of the great *Hindenburg*. The flames spread quickly across the zeppelin's shell, reaching through to ignite its hydrogen supply with a final, crippling explosion.

As the *Hindenburg* crumpled toward the ground, landing crews on the ground fled in terror and passengers aboard the ship leapt to their deaths. In just thirty-four seconds, the ship was reduced to a twisted, burning heap of debris. Thirty-five passengers and crew members and one victim on the ground perished in the blaze.

Within minutes, local radio stations in New York and New Jersey were flashing bulletins of the crash, but it is Herb Morrison's eyewitness account of the horrifying tragedy that remains inextricably associated with the event. Overcome by shock and disbelief, Morrison began describing the indescribable:

"It's burning, bursting into flames and is falling on the mooring mast and all the folks, we—this is one of the worst catastrophes in the

*"It's a terrific crash…
There's smoke and there's
flames…the fires are
crashing to the ground….
Oh, the humanity!"*

Left to right:
A small spark triggered
the explosion of the
hydrogen-filled
Hindenburg over
Lakehurst, New Jersey.
Thirty-five of the ninety-
seven passengers died

world! It's a terrific sight. Oh, the humanity and
all the passengers!"

Expert opinion is that a spark caused by static
electricity ignited hydrogen seeping from a rup-
tured gas bag. Regardless of the cause and the
steps that may have prevented it, the catastrophe
of the *Hindenburg* marked the end of passenger
zeppelins. But even as Herb Morrison's chilling
eyewitness report chronicled the end of one era, it
signaled the beginning of another—an age in
which electronic media would routinely report
shocking events in the moment they occur.

Pearl Harbor
Under Attack

December 7
1941

Left to right:
Pearl Harbor during the
Japanese attack • Japanese
bombers hit the USS
Shaw. In total, eighteen
ships were sunk
or damaged

*Nobody now fears that a Japanese fleet could deal an
unexpected blow on our Pacific possessions....Radio
makes surprise impossible.*
—Josephus Daniels, former U.S. Secretary
of the Navy, October 16, 1922

In the years prior to World War II, political tensions had been mounting between the United
States and Japan. The Japanese economy had been
battered by the worldwide recession that began in
the late 1920s. Japanese nationalism was on the
rise and a strong military-industrial complex was
building. It was, perhaps, not surprising that Japan
looked to foreign expansion as a cure for its economic woes. By 1937, Japan was involved in an
undeclared but fierce war with China. The United
States did not act until 1940 when it terminated
its existing commercial treaty with Japan, thereby
imperiling Japanese access to critical raw materials.

Elements of the U.S. Fleet were moved to Pearl
Harbor and the command was renamed the U.S.
Pacific Fleet. Japan formally allied with the Axis
when it signed the Tripartite Pact with Germany
and Italy in 1940. Partly in response to this agree-
ment, the U.S. increased its aid to Nationalist
China. Japan continued its military forays into
Southeast Asia while negotiating with the U.S. to
normalize trading relations. In July 1941, Japan
effectively seized control of French Indo-China.
Two days later, the U.S. government froze all
Japanese assets, thus eliminating trade with Japan.

During the remainder of 1941, the U.S. and
Japan were in tense negotiations to restore trade
and find some formula for co-existence in the
Western Pacific. The Japanese were confronted
with the stark choice of either giving up their
expansionist plans in exchange for a lifting of the
U.S. embargo or going to war. In November 1941,
the decision was made that it would be war

"No matter how long it may take us to overcome this premeditated invasion, the American people...will win through to absolute victory."

unless a diplomatic solution to the embargo could be reached that would not seriously hamper Japan's expansion.

Admiral Yamamoto, Commander-in-Chief of the Japanese Combined Fleet, devised a bold plan to simultaneously attack U.S. and British possessions in the Western Pacific. The war would start with a strike at Pearl Harbor that was intended to eliminate the U.S. Pacific Fleet, particularly its aircraft carriers. A near simultaneous attack would be launched on the Philippines and on Hong Kong, with other incursions following rapidly across Southeast Asia. The Japanese hoped that the U.S. would be unwilling or unable to support a two-front war and would give precedence to the European conflict, allowing Japan ample time to secure its Western Pacific empire.

Six Japanese carriers set sail on November 26, staying well north of the shipping lanes and so reaching the Hawaiian Islands without being observed. At 6:00 a.m. on December 7, 1941, the first Japanese wave of 183 planes took off through thick cloud cover from aircraft carriers 275 miles north of Oahu. At 7:02 a.m. local time, army radar operations on Oahu's north shore picked up the approaching Japanese aircraft, but mistook them for incoming U.S. B-17 bombers. The first Japanese bomb was dropped at

7:55 a.m. on Wheeler Field; minutes later bombs and torpedoes were striking ships anchored in Pearl Harbor. The second wave of dive-bombers and high-level bombers struck at 8:40 a.m.

The attack was sudden and devastating. The U.S. battleships, seven in a neat row in the center of the harbor and the other in dry dock, were the primary targets. All eight were seriously damaged, with four sinking, including the *Arizona* and the *Oklahoma*. Ten other ships were sunk or disabled, almost two hundred aircraft were destroyed, and over twenty-four hundred people were killed. The Japanese losses were light, twenty-nine aircraft and perhaps one hundred lives. The three U.S. aircraft carriers stationed at Pearl Harbor were, by good luck, at sea and escaped damage. These carriers played a decisive role in the coming war.

While battle raged in the Pacific, Sunday, December 7, 1941, passed in the rest of the United States much like any other day. America's football fans were listening as the Dodgers were leading the Giants 7-0 in a playoff. NBC was broadcasting a program called National Vespers, while the New York Philharmonic aired live over the Columbia Broadcasting System. Suddenly, at 2:26 p.m. eastern standard time, the Mutual Broadcasting System suspended their play-by-play of the Giants–Dodgers game with the

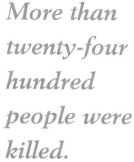

More than twenty-four hundred people were killed.

announcement: "Ladies and gentlemen, we interrupt this broadcast to bring you an important bulletin from the United Press. Flash! Washington—The White House announces a Japanese attack on Pearl Harbor. Stay tuned for further developments to be broadcast as they are received." Later that afternoon, a reporter from station KTU, the NBC affiliate in Honolulu, managed to climb atop the Advertiser Publisher Company building and file one of the first eyewitness reports of the devastation. Interruptions in local broadcasting and bulletins continued throughout the day.

The next day, the Japanese attacked American and British posts throughout the Pacific, including the Philippines. President Roosevelt, rallying the country in front of an emergency joint session of Congress, formally declared war. On December 11, honoring the Tripartite Treaty, Germany and Italy declared war on the United States. In one of the most colossal strategic blunders of modern warfare, neither Adolph Hitler nor Admiral Yamamoto believed that the U.S. would play any significant role in the war it was being forced to join.

Left to right:
The attack left Pearl Harbor with 188 planes destroyed and 159 damaged • The USS *Cassin* and the USS *Downes* also fell victim to the attack • Destruction of Pearl Harbor as seen from a nearby farm

D-Day
The Normandy Invasion

June 6
1944

Well before America entered World War II, Germany had occupied most of Europe and was building a militarized and fortified stronghold for a Third Reich they believed destined to rule the world for a thousand years or more. The Allies knew that if Hitler ever established this vast domain there would be little room for democratic governments anywhere in the world. To the Allies, this war was truly a war for the future of all humanity and there could be no victory that left Germany in control of Europe.

General Dwight David "Ike" Eisenhower was a protégé of army chief of staff General George C. Marshall and an early proponent of a direct European assault. Years before the cross-channel invasion, he mapped out its strategy, forewarning that such a huge effort hinged on a commitment from both Britain and the U.S. Plans for a direct assault on Germany by an amphibious assault on the French coast were made as early as 1942, but

the British were unwilling to commit to what they feared would be a replay of the horrible trench warfare of World War I. Instead, the Allies concentrated on Germany's southern periphery, fighting extensive campaigns in Northern Africa and Italy. Eisenhower led seaborne attacks in Morocco and Algiers in 1942, and in Sicily and Italy in 1943, emerging from these campaigns as a proven field general with unmatched experience in the complexities of large-scale amphibious invasions.

Eisenhower's plan for a cross-channel invasion was finally accepted by the Allied command on January 15, 1944, and shortly thereafter Ike arrived in London as Supreme Commander of the Allied Expeditionary Force. Operation Overlord, as it was code-named, was not just an attempt to free parts of France, but a massive onslaught to pierce the heart of Germany and destroy its armed forces. In a few short months, southern

The coast bristled with mines and artillery emplacements.

England became, under Eisenhower's tireless direction, a huge military staging area. The Allies built over one hundred airfields and stockpiled the munitions, food, and fuel that would be required by a force that would quickly number more than one million soldiers and hundreds of thousands of vehicles. Of equal importance, Eisenhower forged Allied military and political leaders into a unified command that could act with single-minded purpose to defeat a German army that would be fighting for its life.

The German High Command was, of course, alert to the threat of a seaborne invasion and, though pre-occupied with the Russian front, began a massive fortification of the entire twelve hundred-mile coastline of Europe. General Rommel inspired and directed this effort, and under his leadership, the European coastline became a formidable barrier. The coast bristled with mines and artillery emplacements which were backed up by trenches, roads, and rail lines to facilitate the rapid movement of infantry and armor. Rommel realized that if the Allied army established a footing on the European shore, the two and one-half million Allied troops waiting in England would pour onto the continent.

Rommel had done his work well and Allied planners realized that a simple frontal assault would be unlikely to work and would be so costly in human life that the Allied army could be fatally weakened. The final plan was to convince the German command that the actual invasion would be in the Pas de Calais region (where the distance between England and the French coast is shortest) rather than one hundred miles further south in Normandy. In addition, over twenty thousand paratroopers were to land hours before the invasion to guard both eastern and western flanks and cut critical rail lines and bridges.

Left to right:
General Dwight D. Eisenhower and Sir Bernard Montgomery monitor pre-Normandy invasion maneuvers • Allied troops reach the Normandy beach near Bernieres • Allied troops pour ashore on the Normandy coast

Nothing worked perfectly, but everything worked well enough, and Allied troops secured the beaches.

By June 5, 1944, the Allied army was poised to strike. Approximately nine thousand ships were either at sea or ready to cast off. High winds and rain were pummeling the coast and channel, but the forecast was for clearing skies and Eisenhower, as Supreme Commander, gave the order to attack. The paratroopers were the first on the ground, landing behind enemy lines shortly after midnight on June 6. The infantry landed on the five Normandy beaches shortly after dawn, with over ten thousand Allied airplanes striking just before to blunt German defenses. Nothing worked perfectly, but everything worked well enough, and courageous Allied troops secured the beaches and sealed the eventual fate of the Third Reich.

Back in the United States, early on Tuesday morning, NBC was broadcasting the accordion, organ, and guitar music of the popular New York night-spot trio, the Three Suns. At 12:41 a.m. eastern standard time, the program was interrupted by a special bulletin reporting that NBC's short-wave monitoring station had just picked up a bulletin from London, credited to the German Transocean News Agency, reporting an Allied invasion had begun. The announcer warned that there was no official confirmation and the network returned to regular programming. (These American listeners actually heard of the invasion many hours before Hitler did because his staff was unwilling to wake him with such news.) Less than two hours later, all the major networks called their news reporters and commentators to their microphones and key operating personnel to their stations. Bulletins continued throughout the night as unconfirmed reports evolved into chilling reality. Finally, at 3:30 a.m., the formal announcement of the Allied invasion was flashed over the air, and for the next twenty-four hours Americans listened intently to event-by-event broadcasts of the largest military operation ever attempted.

The Allied casualties were high at 10,274, but the Allies gained their first foothold in France, and Hitler's days in power were numbered.

Left to right:
A citizen of Ostheim, France, cycles past an American transport in his ruined town. The German army destroyed the town, leaving only the main street intact • British troops use a tank as a blackboard to announce their next strategy • Aftermath of the Normandy invasion

President Roosevelt *Dies*

April 12
1945

Left to right:
President and First Lady
Eleanor Roosevelt, April
1941 • British Prime
Minister Winston
Churchill, FDR, and
Soviet Premier Joseph
Stalin at the Yalta
Conference, 1945 • The
Roosevelts used Little
White House in Warm
Springs, Georgia, as a
place to recuperate from
the duties of Washington.
Roosevelt died here
during a spring vacation

He was the only man to be elected president of the United States four times, and he did it while presiding over two of the greatest crises in American history, the Great Depression and World War II. His policies in office dramatically changed the country socially and economically, while altering the nature of the presidency itself. If ever a man was made for the times, it was Franklin Delano Roosevelt.

Though he grew up in wealthy surroundings, he was dedicated to reform on behalf of the poor. Physically crippled by polio, he exuded confidence and vitality as he led the country through many of its darkest hours. And the nation responded in kind, re-electing him to office by wide margins of victory—even when, in 1944, his failing health suggested that he might not live long enough to complete his term. As long as the U.S. remained at war with Germany and Japan, the American people were determined to stick by their commander-in-chief.

By March 1945, with victory in Europe nearly at hand, Franklin Roosevelt had been president for more than twelve years, but the war and the office were taking their toll on his health. Recognizing his ailing condition, Roosevelt decided to leave for a vacation to the Little White House in Warm Springs, Georgia, a spot that usually improved his health. He arrived there on the afternoon of March 30.

The Georgia air seemed to invigorate the President, and soon he settled into a balanced routine of work and pleasure.

On Monday, April 9, Lucy Rutherford, accompanied by her painter friend, Elizabeth Shoumatoff, arrived to spend the final week of the vacation with the President. Lucy and Roosevelt met when he was assistant secretary of the navy, and FDR became quite smitten with her. Lucy brought Shoumatoff with her to paint a portrait of Roosevelt during their stay.

On April 11, Roosevelt worked on a draft of his upcoming Jefferson Day speech, well-crafted words and sentiments that would mirror his faith in the American spirit: "The only limit to our realization of tomorrow, will be our doubts of today. Let us move forward with strong and active faith."

At noon the following day, Elizabeth Shoumatoff began work on FDR's portrait. The President sat in the living room dressed in a double-breasted gray suit and crimson tie. Surrounded by Lucy and several others, Roosevelt sifted through a stack of papers as Shoumatoff sketched.

At around 1:00 p.m. eastern time, the butler brought FDR and his party their lunch. At that moment, Roosevelt seemed agitated and flinched in his chair. An assistant asked the President if he needed help. FDR's head went forward. He gripped his head with his left hand and said,

"Men will thank God on their knees a hundred years from now, that Franklin D. Roosevelt was in the White House."

EXTRA
LATEST WAR NEWS
Los Angeles Times Pictorial

ROOSEVELT DEAD!
Cerebral Hemorrhage Proves Fatal; President Truman Sworn in Office

Yanks Near
Suburb Area
of Berlin

Emergency Cabinet
Session Summoned;
Parley Plan in Doubt

Truman Takes
Oath of Office
as President

Ship Blows Up; U.S. SUBMARINE SCAMP
Hundreds Die AND LARGE LCS LOST

Yanks Storm
Bohol Island

Left to right:
On the morning of April 13, 1945, Americans nationwide woke to papers announcing the sad event • The caisson bearing Roosevelt's body moves toward the White House, April 14, 1945

"I have a terrific headache." They would be his final words. The President collapsed and lost consciousness.

The President's physician, Dr. Bruenn, who had accompanied him to Warm Springs, was summoned to the President's bedroom, where he had been moved. Roosevelt struggled to survive, but his breathing had stopped. Despite desperate attempts at artificial respiration and a shot of adrenaline into his heart, the President was pronounced dead at 3:35 p.m.

By 5:30 p.m., Vice President Harry Truman arrived at the White House. When Mrs. Eleanor Roosevelt told him of the President's death, he asked her if there was anything he could do for her. Knowing the magnitude of the job before him, she reciprocated, "Is there anything we can do for you?" Within ninety minutes, the Cabinet had been assembled, and Harry S. Truman became the thirty-third president of the United States.

Meanwhile, the nation began to hear of the tragic news with flashes starting at 5:47 p.m. eastern time. *Tom Mix* listeners on the Mutual Broadcasting System and children listening to the Daniel Boone serial *Wilderness Road* on CBS were jolted by broadcast interruptions announcing Roosevelt's death. People of every walk of life struggled to come to terms with it. For the millions who adored him, an America without Roosevelt seemed almost inconceivable. The *New York Times* was munificent in its editorial statement: "Men will thank God on their knees a hundred years from now, that Franklin D. Roosevelt was in the White House."

FDR's battles were over, and within a month, the country he served for so long would end its long fight by claiming victory in Europe.

V-E Day
War in Europe Ends

May 7
1945

Left to right:
Adolf Hitler and Eva Braun committed suicide in his Berlin bunker shortly after their wedding • Soviet troops in the Kolonenstrasse, Berlin, during the Allied offensive • In a show of triumph, Soviet troops raise the hammer and sickle flag atop Reichs Chancellory, Berlin, May 2, 1945

By mid-April 1945, the Allied powers were drawing nearer to victory in Europe and the Pacific. Russian forces were within thirty-five miles of Berlin, Hitler's Third Reich headquarters. Meanwhile, the U.S. and British troops had captured Nuremberg, and were less than two hundred miles away. General Dwight D. Eisenhower, the Supreme Allied Commander, made the decision not to march on the city, instead allowing the Russian army to capture the German capital. In less than a week, Soviet troops had completely surrounded Berlin.

Meanwhile, Hitler and his mistress Eva Braun, along with a small cadre of loyalists, were hidden in an underground bunker where they continued to contemplate new strategies. Hitler refused to believe that his armies could be losing. Despite his delusions of holding back the advancing Allied forces, the sounds of the Russian army marching overhead told a different story. Having named

Grand Admiral Karl Doenitz as his successor, Adolf Hitler married Braun and the two committed suicide in his Berlin bunker on April 30.

On May 2, in a show of triumph, Russian soldiers flew their red hammer and sickle flag atop the landmarks of a Berlin in ruins. Grand Admiral Doenitz, not wanting Germany to fall under Russian control, attempted to surrender only to the Western Allies but was refused. Finally, on May 7, 1945, Germany surrendered unconditionally.

The British Ministry of Information was first to hear the news of the surrender in a German radio broadcast. The statement broadcast to the German people was attributed to the German Foreign Minister who said simply, "German men and women, the High Command of the Armed Forces has today, at the order of Grand Admiral Doenitz, declared the unconditional surrender of all fighting German troops." The bulletin was

"Our rejoicing is sobered…by a supreme consciousness of the terrible price we have paid to rid the world of Hitler and his evil band."

relayed to the Allies, and was flashed via radio across the U.S.

In his formal announcement an hour later from the White House, President Truman said that his only wish was "that Franklin D. Roosevelt had lived to witness this day." He went on to say that "our rejoicing is sobered and subdued by a supreme consciousness of the terrible price we have paid to rid the world of Hitler and his evil band." Truman concluded by reminding the nation that "the victory won in the west, must now be won in the east."

Europe lay in ruins. For the second time in thirty years, much of the world had mobilized to defeat Germany's war machine. For the nations occupied by German troops, the horror was insurmountable. As Allied forces battled their way to Berlin, they began liberating the survivors of Nazi concentration camps. The hundreds of camps were at first constructed to house Hitler's political opponents and then to enslave Jews, Gypsies, and prisoners of war. Collectively, they could hold as many as one million people at a given time, subjecting prisoners of varied educational, ethnic, and religious backgrounds to starvation, slave labor, and torture. Hitler used these as an aid to his "final solution," a plan to eliminate all European Jewish citizens. Larger camps, such as Poland's Auschwitz, were equipped to kill up to twelve hundred people daily. The total death toll from Nazi concentration camps ranges as high as eleven million people—six million of whom were Jews.

More than half the military deaths of the war came on the eastern front, primarily due to the clash between Germany and Russia. Germany lost 3,250,000 soldiers with Russia suffering more than six million military casualties. U.S. casualties totaled more than 400,000, and the British and the French each lost 250,000 soldiers. Worldwide, an estimated fifty-five million people lost their lives as a result of the Second World War.

Determined not to let it happen again, the Allied forces partitioned Germany into two separate states, east and west. Yet, this partition would itself become the focus of a new kind of global conflict—the cold war—for decades to come.

Left to right:
An American soldier accepts a gift from a cheerful resident of the newly liberated Luxeuil, France, 1944 • Thousands of Parisians celebrate V-E Day on the Boulevard des Capucines, May 1945 • Citizens of Bourg, France, cheer as American troops of the 7th Army, 45th Division, march through town, September 4, 1944

"The victory won in the west, must now be won in the east."

Atomic Bomb
Destroys Hiroshima

August 6
1945

Construction of the atomic bomb lasted two and one-half years and cost $2 billion. The ultimate cost, however, would impact the globe. Following its successful test in the New Mexico desert just before dawn on July 16, 1945, Brigadier General Thomas F. Farrell, stunned by what he had just witnessed, reacted simply by saying, "The war is over." In thirty days his statement proved to have been prophetic.

The idea for building an atomic bomb began with a letter from Albert Einstein to President Franklin Roosevelt in August 1939. Einstein wrote at the time about the possibility of developing a fission bomb of extraordinary annihilative capacity. In 1943, anxious to expedite an Allied victory, Roosevelt decided to test Einstein's theory. He assembled an elite group of scientists headed by Dr. J. Robert Oppenheimer, gave it the code-name Manhattan Project, and set them

to work at a secret government facility in Los Alamos, New Mexico.

President Harry Truman was in the Berlin suburb of Potsdam, Germany, meeting with leaders of the Allied nations when he received confirmation of the successful bomb testing. For the President, the decision of dropping the bomb was a non-issue—the ends certainly justified the means. After meeting with Truman about the bomb, Winston Churchill explained the need for such utter destruction: "to bring the war to an end, to give peace to the world…by a manifestation of overwhelming power at the cost of a few explosions seemed, after all our toils and perils, a miracle of deliverance."

On July 24, 1945, Truman ordered the uranium-based bomb, now code-named Little Boy, sent to the Air Force. Components of Little Boy arrived two days later aboard the U.S. warship

"The Japanese war began with their attack on Pearl Harbor. They have been repaid many-fold."

Indianapolis in Tinian, an island located some sixteen hundred miles south of Japan. Air Force Lieutenant Colonel Paul W. Tibbets and over seventeen hundred members of his 509th Composite Group greeted the Indianapolis and its deadly cargo. It was their mission to deliver Little Boy to its target.

That same day, an ultimatum was communicated to Japan in the Potsdam Declaration, issued by the U.S., Britain, and Nationalist China. It called for the government of Japan "to proclaim now the unconditional surrender of all Japanese armed forces....The alternative for Japan is prompt and utter destruction."

The Potsdam communiqué arrived in Japan on July 27. Fearing that their revered Emperor Hirohito might be deposed or harmed if they agreed to surrender, and ignorant of the fact that the U.S. possessed nuclear capability, the Japanese

Far left to right:
Dr. J. Robert Oppenheimer • The 20,000-foot high smoke column above Hiroshima, Japan, August 6, 1945 • B-29 bomber *Enola Gay* • Aerial view of Hiroshima prior to the bombing

Left to right:
A young bombing survivor • Destruction from the atomic bomb 550 feet from ground zero • An injured mother and child after the bomb

leaders decided to reject the Potsdam Declaration and vowed to continue fighting.

Japan's rejection of the Potsdam Declaration pointed American officials to the other side of the ultimatum. Truman cabled Secretary of War Henry Stimson from Potsdam authorizing him to drop the bomb. On the afternoon of August 5, Little Boy was hoisted into the bomb bay of the *Enola Gay*, the B-29 named in honor of commander Tibbets' mother. The nearly nine-thousand-pound uranium bomb was ten feet long, twenty-eight inches in diameter, and contained the equivalent of twenty thousand tons of dynamite. On August 6, at 2:45 a.m. local time, the *Enola Gay* departed on its historic and deadly mission.

The crew of *Enola Gay* reached its destination at 8:15 a.m. Hiroshima and its citizens had little warning other than the sound of the approaching planes. Little Boy exploded 1,850 feet above Hiroshima, creating a blinding flash and

Atomic Bomb Destroys Hiroshima

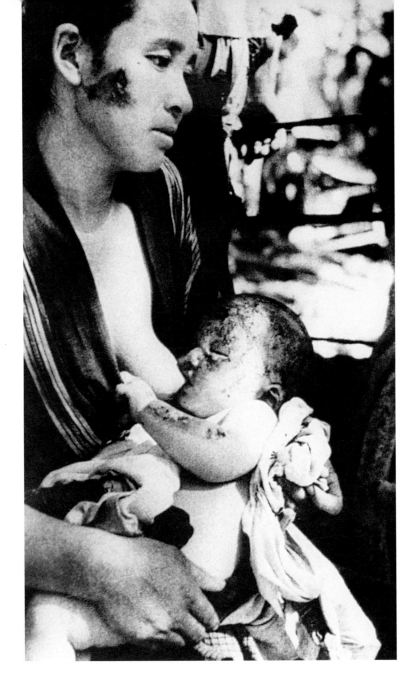

The damage inflicted upon Hiroshima was almost beyond imagining.

victims. A shock wave with an equivalent force of 12,500 tons of TNT obliterated the buildings that were left standing after the initial blast.

Approximately eighty thousand Japanese and twenty-three American prisoners of war died within an hour of the explosion. Eventually, another one hundred thirty thousand Japanese would die from radiation-related illnesses.

America first learned of the existence of the atomic bomb sixteen hours after it had been dropped on Hiroshima. Many Americans were tuned in to the popular Fred Waring program when it was interrupted for the reading of a statement released by President Truman, saying, "An American airplane dropped one bomb on Hiroshima, an important Japanese army base. The Japanese war began with their attack on Pearl Harbor. They have been repaid many-fold."

On August 9, the U.S. dropped one more atomic bomb, this time over Nagasaki, Japan. This blow, coupled with a recent Soviet declaration of war against them, left Japan in a very weakened position. After gaining Allied assurance that Hirohito could maintain emperor status, Japan finally conceded. At noon on August 15, a message recorded by Emperor Hirohito was broadcast throughout Japan. His was a voice most Japanese were hearing for the first time. The Emperor informed the Japanese people that "the enemy has begun to employ a new and most cruel bomb, the power of which to do damage is indeed incalculable, taking the toll of many innocent lives." With that, Japan surrendered.

temperatures as hot as seventy-two hundred degrees Fahrenheit. At the hypocenter, buildings boiled and melted, rivers burned, and people vaporized into thin air, leaving only shadows of their images imprinted on the smoldering landscape. Further away, survivors searched for first aid or loved ones, some trailing flesh as they stumbled through the radioactive debris. Heat from Little Boy's mushroom cloud condensed water vapor that resulted in black rain—marble-shaped, radioactive drops that severely scarred its

Japan Surrenders
WWII Ends

Left to right:
The atomic destruction of Nagasaki, Japan • Japanese officials, some in formal mourning attire, arrive onboard the USS *Missouri* in Tokyo Bay for surrender ceremonies, September 2, 1945 • General Yoshira Umeza signs the surrender document while General MacArthur and Lieutenant General Sutherland watch

America's war in the Pacific began after Japan's surprise attack on the U.S. naval station of Pearl Harbor, Hawaii, on December 7, 1941, and raged for nearly four years. It came to a gruesome and exacting end when, as President Harry S. Truman put it, "we harnessed the basic power of the universe…and loosed it against those who brought war to the Far East." The final human toll was unprecedented. Not since the Black Death in the fourteenth century had so many people been killed, wounded, displaced, or had their lives so completely changed. If the Second World War was the century's turning point, then the turning point for war was the decision to utilize the atomic bomb.

By mid-1945, with victory in Europe at hand, the Allied forces set their sights on a carefully developed strategy for a land invasion of Japan code-named Operation Downfall. It was intended to strike at Japan's key military points,

incapacitating enemy capabilities. The plan was ultimately scrapped for two reasons: the anticipation of fierce resistance and losses of a million men or more, and the sudden availability of a secret weapon—the atomic bomb—capable of wreaking unimaginable destruction.

While Truman saw the bomb as "the most terrible thing ever discovered," he also saw it as being the most useful, and ordered its immediate construction and deployment.

On July 26, the U.S., Britain, and Nationalist China issued the Potsdam Declaration, which called for Japan's unconditional surrender. Japan rejected the offer, however, fearing that such a complete surrender would jeopardize the life of Emperor Hirohito. Officials had no idea that the U.S. was prepared to launch such a deadly attack. The Japanese vowed to keep fighting, believing the damage and losses of future battles could not surpass those already fought. They were wrong.

*"Flash—Japanese surrender.
The war is over!"*

On August 6, 1945, at 8:15 a.m., the atomic bomb, code-named Little Boy, was dropped on the Japanese city of Hiroshima, releasing an unearthly heat of up to seventy-two hundred degrees Fahrenheit, instantly vaporizing everything within four square miles of its hypocenter. The death toll numbered in the hundreds of thousands.

The American people first learned of the bombing of Hiroshima, and of U.S. nuclear capability, from a White House bulletin that was flashed over radio that evening. Japanese radio reported that Hiroshima "suffered considerable damage as a result of an attack by a few B-29s. Our enemies have apparently used a new type of bomb. The details are being investigated." Tokyo knew little of what had happened to Hiroshima; damage was so great that communication in and around the area had virtually shut down. Washington had hoped for an immediate surrender, but the bombing merely stunned Japanese officials.

Official word of the war's end would not come until the next evening. But that did not stop war-weary Americans from pouring into the streets to celebrate.

Despite the horror of Hiroshima, the shocked Japanese leadership vowed to fight on, convinced that America had only one bomb. On August 9, a B-29 carrying the second atomic bomb, Fat Man, headed for the targeted city of Korkura. Experiencing cloud cover and low fuel, the pilot, Major Charles W. Sweeney, was forced to change his course for an emergency landing on nearby Okinawa, dropping his deadly cargo instead on the alternate target of Nagasaki on the way. The power unleashed by Fat Man was nearly double that of Little Boy, killing forty thousand of the city's inhabitants instantly.

News of Nagasaki reached Japan's Supreme War Council as insult added to injury. The night before, the U.S.S.R. had abruptly declared war on Japan. Just as Nagasaki was destroyed by the U.S., Soviet troops attacked Japanese-held Manchuria.

Despite the devastation of the atomic bombs and the unexpected Soviet invasion, the six-member Supreme Council remained deadlocked on the issue of surrender. After eight hours, Prime Minister Suzuki made the unprecedented decision to turn to Emperor Hirohito. The Japanese believed that the Emperor was god-like, and beyond the process of debating public policy. But the Emperor spoke firmly, stating that "continuing the war means destruction for the nation and a

Opposite page:
Crowds gather in
Times Square,
New York,
to celebrate
Japanese surrender,
August 15, 1945

prolongation of bloodshed and cruelty in the world....We must bear the unbearable. I swallow my tears and give my sanction to the proposal to accept the Allied proclamation."

At noon Japanese time on August 15, over Japanese radio, Hirohito announced Japan's acceptance of the terms of surrender. It was after midnight in the U.S., but many were awake listening to a live remote broadcast of Cab Calloway and his band on the Mutual Broadcasting System. The broadcast was suddenly interrupted with a "flash" that all America had been waiting to hear, "Japanese radio has just been heard announcing the acceptance of surrender terms. The war is over!" Official word of the war's end would not come until the next evening at 7:00 p.m., when the Japanese surrender was formally received at the White House. But that did not stop war-weary Americans from pouring into the streets to celebrate the end of World War II.

Three weeks later, on September 2, 1945, aboard the new battleship *Missouri*, named for President Truman's home state, Japanese officials dressed in formal mourning attire, led by Mamoru Shigemitsu, surrendered to representatives of the Allied powers, led by General Douglas MacArthur. Thus ended the worst war the world had ever seen.

Truman Defeats *Dewey*

November 3
1948

He was a man who became president by stepping into shoes that were nearly impossible to fill. His predecessor, Franklin Delano Roosevelt, was everything Harry S. Truman was not—rich and well-educated, a man who exuded aristocratic confidence by identifying with the common man. Truman was that common man, a small-town businessman who had been elected to the Senate in Missouri, and later selected as Roosevelt's vice president. But when Roosevelt died, it was left to Truman to hold the reins of leadership, and to make one difficult decision after the next, from dropping atomic bombs on Japan to presiding over the economic depression which followed the war's end.

By 1948, Truman was eligible to run for election in his own right, but he barely managed to receive the nomination of his own Democratic party. His chief opponent in the general election was New York Governor Thomas E. Dewey, a longtime presidential hopeful.

Despite having held the office of president since Roosevelt's death in 1945, Truman was a serious underdog. Nearly two months before votes were cast, the highly respected Roper Poll felt a Truman loss was certain and ceased tracking voters' preferences. A *Newsweek* poll of fifty top political writers unanimously predicted a Dewey victory, and sixty-five percent of editorials in the country's newspapers, including most major ones, backed him. The *Chicago Daily Tribune*, in an editorial that would only amplify its

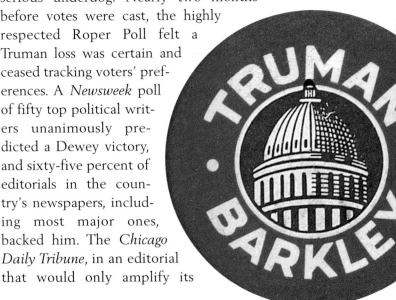

later embarrassment, called Truman "an incompetent." Even gambling bookies held long odds against him.

Having been defeated by Roosevelt in the 1944 presidential election in part due to his attack strategy, Dewey was content to avoid controversy on the campaign trail. Truman, meanwhile, embarked on a cross country "whistle-stop" campaign speaking to the American people—the laborers, farmers, and common folk with whom he identified. Traveling into the heart of historically Republican-held areas, he delivered fiery attacks targeted at the Republican-controlled Congress from the back of a train.

As the campaign continued, the crowds grew to huge, animated throngs, beseeching Harry to "give 'em hell." The tide was turning, but still, election experts remained skeptical.

On Tuesday, November 2, 1948, Truman and his family voted in Independence, Missouri. In the evening, he skirted away to Excelsior Springs, Missouri, to stay at the Elms Hotel, thereby avoiding the media. He went to bed early, while election results began to trickle in.

The next morning, despite the prognostications of the political experts and pundits, he had received 303 electoral votes, and a four-year ticket to the White House. His Democratic party even regained control of Congress on his coattails.

While network radio and television were able to instantly flash the news that Truman had won, the print media was one step behind. Truman boarded the train and headed back to Washington, D.C. But during a brief stop in St. Louis, he was presented with a copy of the *Chicago Daily Tribune* printed prior to the final votes being counted—the headline read "Dewey Defeats Truman."

The 1948 presidential campaign became the stuff of political legend. By 1952, more sophisticated polling techniques had begun to remove the possibility of such surprises from presidential elections, and campaign by television commercial gradually replaced the grueling physical campaign of travel by train. Despite, or perhaps because of that, the legacy of Harry Truman's "give 'em hell" campaign will remain forever secure.

While network radio and television were able to instantly flash the news that Truman had won, the print media was one step behind.

Chicago Daily Tribune

DEWEY DEFEATS TRUMAN

Left to right:
Truman/Barkley campaign button, 1948 • Truman displays an issue of the *Chicago Daily Tribune* during a stop in St. Louis. The newspaper inaccurately reported the election's outcome • Thomas E. Dewey (left) speaks to Italian journalists before the election

General MacArthur *Fired*

April 11

1951

General Douglas MacArthur was a cele-brated and imperious commander with no shortage of self-regard. Harry S. Truman, whose motto was "the buck stops here," was a president who could not be intimidated. In the midst of the Korean War, the irresistible force met the immov-able object.

Korea had been parceled into two countries after World War II, with a border arbitrarily created about halfway in between, at the 38th lat-itudinal parallel. The Soviet Union oversaw a communist government in North Korea; the U.S. supported a facsimile of democracy in South Korea. In fact, both countries were ruled by lead-ers who wished to take over the other's domain. When North Korea invaded South Korea in 1950, President Truman committed American troops to that country's defense without asking Congress for an official declaration of war, calling Korea "a police action." But it was a war—one that would

last three years and claim over thirty thousand American lives.

For a time, with General MacArthur in command, the allied effort went well, as U.S.-backed armies pushed North Korean forces back beyond the 38th parallel. But despite their mil-itary successes, the Truman–MacArthur rela-tionship was acrimonious at best. MacArthur was prone to displays of maverick behavior and publicly critical of the President's policies. When MacArthur pushed on toward the Chinese border, Chinese troops helped North Korea stage an overwhelming counterattack, turning visions of imminent victory into disaster and defeat. MacArthur vilified the administra-tion for not allowing him to launch a full-scale invasion of China. In April 1951, in a letter read before Congress by Representative Joseph Martin, MacArthur railed against Truman's attempts at peace in Asia. "If we lose the war to

"Old soldiers never die, they just fade away."

Communism in Asia, the fall of Europe is inevitable.... There is no substitute for victory," the General wrote.

It was a clear impertinence to Truman's leadership and command, and the President had heard enough. Supported by a unanimous vote of his Joint Chiefs of Staff, President Truman relieved the insubordinate yet extremely popular general of his command on April 11.

Bulletins immediately flashed the news of MacArthur's firing. Segments of Congress and several newspapers cried for Truman's impeachment, while others wondered what took him so long. A surprised country divided sharply on the issue. Although angry mail poured into the White House, many felt Truman had acted on the necessary principle of upholding the Constitution.

Truman took to the airwaves himself to describe his policies in Korea to the American people. His message expressed great admiration for the general the public loved, while at the same time explaining the necessity of his removal from the Korean campaign.

But MacArthur would have the last word. On April 19, 1951, he returned to Washington to deliver an emotional and eloquent farewell speech before a joint session of Congress, broadcast by radio and television to the rest of the nation. He spoke in fond remembrance of his long career of serving his country, and concluded with a quote from a popular old military barracks ballad, "Old soldiers never die, they just fade away."

Plagued by low public approval ratings and a war that seemed to drag on, Harry Truman would choose not to run for re-election in 1952. America chose a general in his place—D-Day Commander Dwight D. Eisenhower. Yet, it would still take another year before the Korean War finally ground to an uneasy stalemate.

Above:
General Douglas MacArthur and President Harry Truman could not resolve their differences over Korean War policies. MacArthur's public criticism of Truman's judgment left the President with no choice but to fire his maverick general

Sputnik Launched *by Soviets*

October 4
1957

Above:
The second Soviet satellite, *Sputnik II*, entered orbit on November 3, 1957. It is shown here on a test launch

In 1957, the cold war between the U.S. and the Soviet Union reached beyond politics and into outer space. In the years following World War II, the U.S. had become the scientific and technological leader of the free world. Maintaining this pre-eminence was widely believed to be essential to U.S. economic vitality and the best way to contain Soviet aggression. "American ingenuity" in engineering and applied science was recognized throughout the world.

However, the U.S. scientific community was heavily laced with Europeans who had fled the war and post-war devastation and there was concern that U.S. successes were not home-grown accomplishments but based on borrowed European talent. This uncertainty was particularly acute because many believed even the U.S. space program's limited success could be attributed to German scientists who had worked on Hitler's ballistic missile project.

In preparation for the International Geophysical Year (1957-1958), both the U.S. and the Soviet Union announced plans to launch artificial satellites. The U.S. space program was conducted in full view of the world and was obviously struggling. The Soviet space program was centered in a remote region of Kazhakhstan and conducted with utmost secrecy. Rumors of a new launch vehicle, significantly larger than anything the U.S. had built, circulated at scientific meetings. However, even these vague claims were received skeptically and usually dismissed as Soviet propaganda. The Soviet announcement in the summer of 1957 of the frequencies on which their satellite would broadcast was largely ignored.

On October 4, 1957, the Soviets stunned the world when *Sputnik* (literally "traveling companion") rode into orbit on a ballistic missile. By U.S. standards, *Sputnik* was huge; at 184.3 pounds, it was twenty times larger than

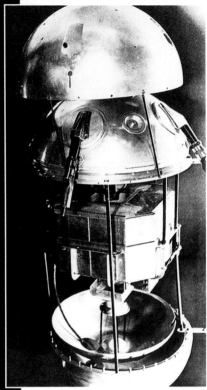

"Today, there is a new moon in the sky."

the satellite the U.S. was attempting to launch. A month later, the Soviet Union compounded U.S. discomfort by launching *Sputnik II* with a live dog named Laika as a passenger. The U.S. failure to launch its small satellite in December of that year emphasized the magnitude of the Soviet accomplishment.

The Soviet success and American failure not only hurt American pride, but also appeared to directly challenge the U.S. ability to curb the Soviets by way of superior technology. While *Sputnik*'s broadcast of eerie intermittent croaking was not a direct threat to national security, the

implied superiority of the Soviets in ballistic missile technology was alarming. To Americans who were primed to believe the worst after a decade of cold war, it was chilling to realize that if this piece of "Soviet propaganda" was true, other secret and even more frightening Soviet initiatives might surface at any time.

The Soviet *Sputnik* successes, with their implication of Soviet scientific and engineering prowess, helped to create not only the huge American space program of the 1960s and 1970s but also spurred U.S. investment in education and scientific research.

Left to right: Sputnik I • Exploded view of Sputnik I showing satellite's interior

John Glenn
Orbits Earth

On April 12, 1961, Soviet cosmonaut Yuri Alekseyevich Gagarin became the first man to orbit the earth. On May 5, 1961, Navy Commander Alan Shepard squeezed into a tiny capsule to hurtle 115 miles above the earth and then parachute back into the Atlantic Ocean less than fifteen minutes later. Captain Virgil "Gus" Grissom completed another sub-orbital flight on July 21, 1961, adding some last-minute drama as he barely escaped drowning when his capsule sank. The Soviets widened their space race lead further when, on August 7, 1961, Gherman Titov completed a twenty-five-hour, seventeen-orbit flight. President Kennedy upped the ante by pledging to put a man on the moon within the decade. For a generation that had grown up reading science fiction, this real-life race into space was irresistible.

Presidential bravado aside, NASA knew that before they could send a man to the moon, they

had to successfully send one into orbit. That man would be Marine Corps Lieutenant Colonel John Glenn.

Glenn's *Mercury* flight, dubbed *Friendship 7*, was plagued by delays. It had been postponed nine times in the two months preceding the launch due to bad weather and last-minute technical glitches. Finally, on February 20, 1962, despite dubious weather conditions over Cape Canaveral, John Glenn woke at 2:20 a.m. eastern standard time, ate breakfast, underwent a brief medical exam, put on his pressure suit, and climbed into the spacecraft.

As the countdown proceeded on schedule, some one hundred thousand spectators gathered on nearby Florida beaches to witness the historic flight and millions more watched the live television coverage. In New York's Grand Central Station, thousands of commuters stared transfixed at CBS television's twelve by sixteen-foot television screen during the final seconds of countdown.

Left to right:
The *Friendship 7* roars into orbit • Grand Central Station television screens provide commuters in New York City a chance to see the liftoff • Glenn awaits blastoff inside the *Friendship 7*

"Godspeed, John Glenn."

As the countdown neared zero, the nation stood in hopeful anticipation, sharing the sentiment expressed by the NASA radio operator who said, "Godspeed, John Glenn." *Friendship 7* cleared the tower at 9:47 a.m. and roared into global orbit.

On the second orbit, the small hydrogen peroxide jets used to maintain the capsule in a stable orientation began to allow large oscillations followed by radical corrections, using much more fuel than the flight plan allowed. A similar problem in the immediately preceding *Mercury* flight (with the chimpanzee Enos as passenger) had caused an early termination. Glenn eventually bypassed the automatic system and assumed manual control. Advocates of manned flight were pleased that the skills of a

human pilot were necessary to successfully complete the mission.

While Glenn appeared to be coping with the attitude-control problem, ground control discovered another, much more serious problem that the human pilot would be helpless to remedy. Telemetry signals suggested that the locking mechanism that held the heat shield in place had not engaged. The fierce heat of re-entry would destroy a spacecraft except for the protection provided by this ceramic heat shield. A package of retro-rockets was strapped to the outside of the heat shield, and it appeared that the shield was being held in place only by this strapping. Ground control feared that when the retro-rockets were discarded, the heat shield also would separate, leaving Glenn in a capsule that would surely burn and disintegrate high in the atmosphere. Ground control decided that the best hope would be to leave the retro-rocket package in place during re-entry. The retro-rockets would, of course, be destroyed, but it was hoped they would last long enough to ensure the heat shield would be held in place by the powerful push of the air generated by the capsule's speed.

Ground control did not inform Glenn that his heat shield might not be locked in place. However, he was asked enough questions about the heat-shield locking mechanism to make him suspicious. When ground control indicated that he might re-enter with the retro-rocket package still attached, he immediately understood and commented that he had heard no sound that indicated a movement of the heat shield during attitude adjustments.

At 2:43 p.m., Glenn fired the breaking rockets. As expected, the retro-rocket package was shortly destroyed, but the heat shield remained in place. *Friendship 7* splashed down about forty miles from its predicted landing site and the destroyer *Noa* quickly recovered the capsule. When *Friendship 7* was examined, it was apparent that the heatshield locking mechanism had worked perfectly, but a small switch had malfunctioned and produced erroneous warning signals.

Glenn had made three orbits in four hours and fifty-five minutes. While the Soviets still had the lead, the U.S. was finally in the race.

Left to right:
Splashdown recovery of *Friendship 7* • President Kennedy and Vice President Johnson listen to Glenn explain his experience

Marilyn Monroe
Dies

August 4 1962

The image of Marilyn Monroe is far more than that of a movie star or a sex symbol—she was an icon for her own generation as well as those to follow. She was not only a premiere movie star of the twentieth century, but one of the most famous women in the history of western civilization. She had fame, wealth, and a legend that endures—and died a shocking death under unexpectedly sordid circumstances still shrouded in mystery and controversy.

Norma Jeane Baker never knew her father. Her mother spent years in an institution, and, at sixteen, Norma Jeane entered an arranged marriage with a family friend. Hers was not a life to be envied.

But, by 1950, the twenty-four-year-old had changed her brown hair to platinum blonde and made her movie debut as Marilyn Monroe. The young actress won the attention of the film industry and the public, and went on to star in such films as *Niagara, Bus Stop, Gentlemen Prefer Blondes, The Seven Year Itch*, and *Some Like It Hot*. Acclaimed for both her comedic talents and her dramatic roles, Marilyn was nevertheless best known for her spectacular, sultry looks and her explosive image as a blonde bombshell.

Movie stars and baseball players are the closest thing America has to royalty, and the fans went crazy in 1954 when Marilyn married baseball great Joe DiMaggio. In spite of her sensational silver screen image, Marilyn was looked upon as a down-to-earth girl who just happened to be gorgeous, famous, and rich. Everybody knew that Joe DiMaggio was a "regular guy," both a man's man and a gentleman. The American public was almost as disappointed as the couple themselves when it turned out that their union was fatally flawed. Marilyn's extreme fame and the demands of her world-famous persona would never let her be the stay-at-home 1950s wife Joltin' Joe had

Marilyn was looked upon as a down-to-earth girl who just happened to be gorgeous, famous, and rich.

bargained for. Both visibly heartbroken, Joe and Marilyn divorced after only nine months.

Her subsequent five-year marriage to intellectual playwright Arthur Miller was no less a failure. Miller's intensity and stability couldn't satisfy Marilyn's need for emotional reassurance, and Miller was reportedly shocked by the extremes of Marilyn's emotional dependence.

By the time of her divorce from Miller in 1961, Marilyn's life was in disarray. She was addicted to prescription sleeping pills and tranquilizers and rumored to be in love affairs with famous men like Frank Sinatra, Bobby Kennedy, and President John F. Kennedy.

In fact, one of Marilyn's more notorious performances was on a nationally telecast birthday salute to President Kennedy. What few knew was that Marilyn had shown up for the

Left to right:
Norma Jeane Baker, a.k.a. Marilyn Monroe, modeled from 1946 to 1948 • Monroe in *The Seven Year Itch*, 1955 • Monroe greets over 10,000 G.I.s in Korea, February 16, 1954

performance with a severe case of sinusitis. Drugged from a mixture of antibiotics and prescribed amphetamines, a nervous Marilyn stood backstage sipping champagne as a seamstress fitted her into a custom-made gown. She was escorted on stage by movie star and Kennedy brother-in-law Peter Lawford. The voluptuous Marilyn half-sang, half-whispered a version of "Happy Birthday" that turned that everyday song into an erotic invitation. It was an incredible performance, and one of her last.

Monroe's death in the late hours of August 4, 1962, continues to spur active discussion. Though her official cause of death is listed as "acute barbiturate poisoning—ingestion of overdose," ideas surrounding the facts of her death are varied.

The ensuing forty years have seen the emergence of nearly as many theories about the "real" story of Marilyn Monroe's death. From discrepancies in autopsy and toxicology reports, numerous theorists have claimed murder at the hands of Kennedy supporters, the Mafia, Jimmy

The ensuing forty years have seen the emergence of nearly as many theories about the "real" story of her death.

Hoffa and the Teamsters, Cuban terrorists, and Soviet communists.

Many believe, as official accounts at the time suggested, that Marilyn Monroe committed suicide—she had already threatened to kill herself on several occasions.

On the other hand, was Marilyn too happy to have killed herself? She had recently reconciled with Joe DiMaggio and had accepted his proposal to marry again. The date was set, her wedding gown ready. Marilyn Monroe was finally going to have the home and family she always wanted—but her dream was destined never to come true.

America was stunned by the shocking news of her death. The thirty-six-year-old actress had managed to combine a sweetness and a sex appeal that enabled her to gain equal popularity with men

and women alike. The death of Marilyn Monroe was a wake-up call for the nation in more ways than one. No, there wasn't always a happy ending. And no, money, fame, and beauty could not buy happiness or love or a home and family.

The day that Joe DiMaggio escorted Marilyn Monroe to her final resting place was August 8, 1962, the date they had set for the renewal of their wedding vows.

Marilyn's death would place her among a revered group of young actors and musicians from her generation whose light was extinguished too soon. With Buddy Holly and James Dean before her, America's fascination with celebrities would crown these young stars with the stature of an idol and an almost cult-like following of fans that endures to this day.

Left to right:
The press crowds Monroe as she leaves the court-house after finalizing her divorce from Arthur Miller • Serenading President Kennedy at his birthday party, 1962 • Twenty years after her death, friends and fans leave flowers at Monroe's crypt in Westwood Cemetery, California

Cuban Missile Crisis
Nuclear War Threatened

October 22
1962

History has not recorded the name of the specific individual charged with interrupting the slumber of President John F. Kennedy on October 16, 1962. The most powerful man in the free world was awakened early that morning to receive aerial reconnaissance photos showing Soviet middle- and intermediate-range nuclear missile launching sites on the island of Cuba, ninety miles south of the United States.

The events of the following thirteen days shook the world and brought it closer to thermonuclear war than ever before or since.

Throughout the summer of 1962, the U.S. had been closely monitoring what it thought might be a significant military buildup in the newly Soviet-aligned Cuba, including the installation of Soviet-backed missile sites. Now, in October, President Kennedy finally had the confirmation he needed to act. Spotted by American

U-2 spy planes, the sites, if armed, could be capable of quickly wiping out U.S. cities.

On October 16, President Kennedy chaired the first of a series of crisis meetings with senior advisors in what he called the Executive Committee of the National Security Council. Options discussed in the Executive Committee meetings included blockade, air strikes, and a full-scale invasion of Cuba. Considering cold war tensions surrounding the recently built Berlin Wall, the President was concerned that a Cuban invasion would result in the Soviet Union seizing Berlin, not to mention looming concerns that any decisions could lead to nuclear holocaust.

At a White House meeting on October 18, 1962, Soviet Foreign Minister Andrei Gromyko informed President Kennedy that all Soviet military assistance in Cuba was solely for defensive purposes. Kennedy responded by strongly warning against Soviet deployment of offensive weapons in Cuba, though he did not yet tip his hand by confirming his awareness of the missiles.

Over the next few days, Kennedy and his Executive Committee continued to debate the risks and possible results of each alternative. On October 21, Kennedy gave his final approval to the "quarantine" plan, consisting of an air and naval blockade which would stop all ships bound for Cuba for boarding and weapons inspection.

The next day, October 22, Kennedy informed the American people of the crisis. Addressing the nation in a televised speech,

Kennedy told a stunned U.S. populace about the Soviet missile sites in Cuba, and outlined his quarantine plan. Further, he warned the Soviets that the U.S. would consider "any nuclear missile launched from Cuba against any nation in the Western Hemisphere as an attack by the Soviet Union on the United States, requiring a full retaliatory attack against the Soviet Union." The world held its breath.

In Cuba, Premier Fidel Castro prepared for war, beginning a massive mobilization of his armed forces and placing his military on its highest alert. More than fourteen thousand American troops

Left to right:
Soviet Premier Nikita Khrushchev greets Cuban Premier Fidel Castro • Aerial photo of a medium-range ballistic missile base, San Cristonal, Cuba

LAUNCH POSITION

MISSILE-READY TENTS

MISSILE ERECTORS

"Any nuclear missile launched from Cuba... [would require] a full retaliatory attack against the Soviet Union."

Left to right:
A U.S. naval destroyer
intercepts a Soviet freighter
off the coast of Cuba •
Fidel Castro • A Soviet ship
departs Cuba with eight
loaded missile transporters •
A worried President
Kennedy speaks to the
nation via television
concerning the crisis

were also called to readiness, and the state of Florida looked like the staging area for world war.

On Wednesday, October 24, Soviet Premier Nikita Khrushchev proposed a summit meeting with Kennedy to discuss ending both the crisis and the threat of nuclear war. At the same time, though, he also was promising to retaliate for the U.S. blockade. Soviet ships, meanwhile, began voluntarily turning away from Cuba. In the words of Secretary of State Dean Rusk, the United States and the Soviet Union were "eyeball to eyeball...the other fellow just blinked."

One day later, the Soviet Premier agreed to a United Nations proposal to suspend both Soviet arms shipments to Cuba and the U.S. blockade for several weeks. He then sent Kennedy a letter proposing that he would declare that his ships were not carrying arms if the U.S. declared that it would not invade Cuba or support other invasion forces. Kennedy

Rudolf Anderson. Anderson was shot down and killed on a routine reconnaissance mission over Cuba, bringing tensions to a fever pitch.

On October 28, 1962, Radio Moscow broadcast a message from the Soviet Premier formally ordering the removal of all Soviet missiles in Cuba in exchange for Kennedy's promise that Cuba would be safe from a U.S. invasion. Though negotiations and missile removal would last for months afterward, Khrushchev's announcement essentially ended the crisis thirteen days after it began. Although repercussions would be felt for some time to come, the immediate threat of nuclear war was past.

The U.S. and the Soviet Union were "eyeball to eyeball...the other fellow just blinked."

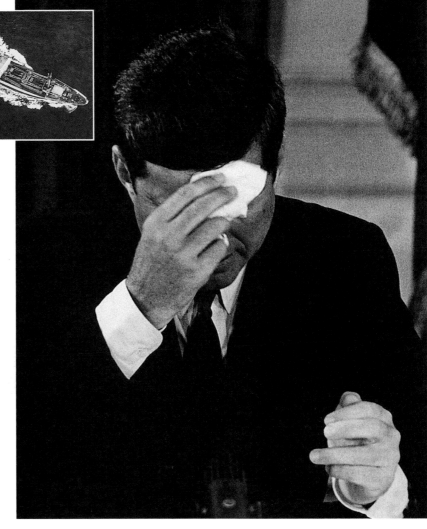

strongly considered both proposals, but gave no firm U.S. acceptance to either the U.N. or Khrushchev. The standoff continued.

Meanwhile, Fidel Castro was in a Cuban bomb shelter cabling to Khrushchev that the American invasion was imminent and proposing pre-emption by inflicting an immediate nuclear strike on the U.S. Castro ordered Cuban anti-aircraft forces to open fire on all U.S. aircraft flying over the island. When Soviet Ambassador to Cuba Aleksandr Alekseyev asked Castro to rescind his order, Castro refused.

Cuban forces would, in fact, fire on U.S. planes, but it was Soviet leaders who would order the attack on the U-2 plane piloted by Major

President Kennedy *Assassinated*

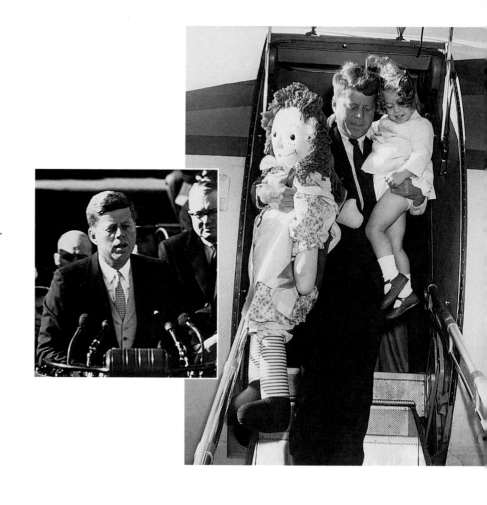

November 22
1963

Left to right:
Kennedy's inauguration,
January 1961
• The President and his
daughter Caroline during
the campaign, October
1960 • The Kennedy
family gathered in its
Hyannisport, Massachusetts,
living room where they
received news that Jack
won the presidency

From the moment he delivered his stirring inaugural address on the bright cold day of January 20, 1961, John F. Kennedy exuded a contagious spirit of freshness and vitality. As president, Kennedy had his share of frustrations and failures, but as a symbol of a generation, he was an unadorned success. Handsome, well-educated, and a decorated war hero, he seemed to symbolize America's optimistic image of itself.

As a politician and leader, television became his great ally, and he used it at every opportunity. Kennedy frequently held televised press conferences, where his spontaneous wit and ready charm were broadcast into the homes of millions. But none of John F. Kennedy's thousand days as president would transfix the nation so dramatically as the one he spent in Dallas, Texas, on November 22, 1963.

Aside from the fact that Kennedy personally enjoyed making public appearances, the Dallas trip was meant as a political fence-mending mission to help shore up his chances for re-election. As an added measure, he decided to bring his vice president, and influential Texan, Lyndon Johnson along on the trip.

The original plan called for Kennedy to spend one day in Texas, visiting Dallas, Fort Worth, San Antonio, and Houston. But two months prior to the trip, the White House decided to extend his visit from the afternoon of November 21 to the evening of November 22, ending with a political fundraising dinner in Austin. The White House also planned a motorcade through downtown Dallas in the hopes that it would evoke a demonstration of the President's personal popularity in a city he had lost in the 1960 election.

Prior to the trip, standard precautions were taken to check with the Secret Service's local Protective Research Section for any potentially dangerous people who might want to harm the

President during his visit. The search turned up no one in the Dallas-Fort Worth territory who could be considered a serious danger.

Air Force One touched down at Love Field in Dallas midmorning on November 22. The picture-perfect day allowed the President and First Lady Jacqueline Kennedy to ride through Dallas in an open-air limousine. Their hosts, the Governor and Mrs. John Connally, rode in the jump seats in front of them. Driving the president's limousine was Secret Service agent William R. Greer, and agent Roy H. Kellerman sat in the front passenger seat. The press vehicle, normally placed ahead of the President's car, was lined up last. Consequently, this prevented any official footage or photos of the tragic event that would take place.

The motorcade left Love Field at approximately 11:50 a.m. destined for the Trade Mart where Kennedy was scheduled to speak at a luncheon in his honor.

Proceeding at eleven miles per hour, the motorcade crawled through the streets of Dallas which were crowded with excited onlookers. By the time the President's car had reached the corner of Houston and Elm Streets in Dealey Plaza, Kennedy had stopped twice to personally greet well-wishers. The motorcade proceeded into downtown Dallas, and into the shadow of the Texas School Book Depository, a seven-story office building and warehouse. Agent Rufus Youngblood, who was riding in the Vice President's car, noticed the clock atop the building

Kennedy seemed to symbolize America's optimistic image of itself.

"Three shots were fired at President Kennedy's motorcade in downtown Dallas. The first reports say that President Kennedy has been seriously wounded."

Clockwise:
Due to pleasant weather, Kennedy insisted that his motorcade car not have its usual protective bubble. He is seated next to wife Jacqueline and behind Texas Governor and Mrs. Connally • A Secret Service member pushes the First Lady back into the presidential car's seat. Jacqueline Kennedy attempted to climb out of the car after her husband had been shot • CBS anchor Walter Cronkite shed tears during his announcement that Kennedy had died • Judge Sarah Hughes administered the oath of office to Lyndon B. Johnson just before Air Force One left Dallas. Jacqueline Kennedy, covered in her husband's blood, looks on

"A flash, apparently official. President Kennedy died at 1:00 p.m."

read 12:30 p.m., the time the motorcade was scheduled to have arrived at the Trade Mart.

Suddenly, the terrifying sound of gunshots ripped through the air. Governor Connally was struck in the shoulder, wrist, and leg. President Kennedy was hit in the neck and back, and finally suffered a massive fatal wound in the rear portion of his head.

The entire attack lasted six to eight seconds. Stunned shock turned to panicked chaos in Dealey Plaza as crowds scattered, running for cover. Agent Greer immediately accelerated the presidential car. Agent Clint Hill, riding on the running board of the follow-up car, jumped onto the back of the limousine where Mrs. Kennedy, stricken with terror, had desperately climbed. Fearing further gunfire, Hill pushed her back into the rear seat, and covered the wounded President and his wife as they raced to Parkland Memorial Hospital four miles away.

When Kennedy died, the optimistic spirit of the "New Frontier" perished with him.

eastern standard time when CBS interrupted its daytime drama *As The World Turns* with only a graphic that read, "CBS News Bulletin." Walter Cronkite reported, "In Dallas, Texas, three shots were fired at President Kennedy's motorcade in downtown Dallas. The first reports say that President Kennedy has been seriously wounded by this shooting." Less than an hour later, an obviously more emotional Cronkite reported the horrible news, "From Dallas, Texas, a flash, apparently official. President Kennedy died at 1:00 p.m. central standard time, two o'clock eastern standard time, some thirty-eight minutes ago."

While television was a relatively young medium, it grew up quickly over the next three and one-half days. Beginning at 1:45 p.m. that fateful Friday afternoon, the three television networks broadcast without interruption for more than seventy hours. The nation watched in collective grief as the slain President was laid to rest.

When John Kennedy died, the optimistic spirit of the "New Frontier" seemed to perish with him; yet, his stature grew to near-mythic proportions. And the turbulence that marked the rest of the 1960s had only just begun.

Left to right:
President Kennedy's coffin moves toward the Capitol Building where his body was placed in state • John F. Kennedy Jr. salutes his father's casket during the funeral outside St. Matthew's Cathedral, November 25, 1963

Within minutes of the shooting, reports began trickling into radio and television stations. Ron Jenkins from radio station KBOX in Dallas was in Dealey Plaza and one of the first to report that "something has happened in the motorcade route." The networks interrupted programming with bulletins of the attack and unconfirmed reports on the President's condition. It was mid-afternoon, and while most Americans first heard the news on the radio, the bulletin that became synonymous with the event came at 1:40 p.m.

Lee Harvey Oswald
Assassinated

November 24

1963

As a young man, Lee Harvey Oswald joined the Marines, becoming a sharpshooter and working with the U-2 reconnaissance program. He was given a hardship discharge in 1959 to tend to his ailing mother, but soon attempted to emigrate to the Soviet Union. He lived in the Soviet Union for two and one-half years, married Marina Prusakova, had a daughter, and returned to the United States with his new family in 1962.

In 1963, Oswald tried once again to secure visas for Cuba and the Soviet Union, but was refused. The Oswald family settled in Dallas, and an acquaintance arranged a job interview for Oswald at the Texas School Book Depository. He was hired to fill book orders for $1.25 an hour.

On the morning of November 22, 1963, Oswald's neighbor, Buell Frazier, drove him to work. Frazier noticed Oswald was carrying a long, brown paper package, but didn't question him about it.

At approximately 12:30 that afternoon, downtown Dallas broke into pandemonium when President Kennedy was fatally shot as his motorcade passed the Texas School Book Depository building in Dealey Plaza. Although witnesses differed in their accounts of the direction from which the sound of the shots emanated, within minutes, police focused on the sixth floor southeast corner window of the depository.

As Oswald was walking out of the depository building following the shooting, an NBC newsman named Robert MacNeil frantically asked Oswald where he could find the nearest phone. Oswald assisted the newsman and then headed for home. He arrived at his rooming house at 1:00 p.m., but left again a short time later.

Howard Brennan, an eyewitness who was standing on Elm Street directly opposite the book depository, provided police with a description of a slender man, about five-feet ten-inches tall, in his early thirties. The Dallas police immediately broadcast an all-points bulletin and description based primarily on Brennan's observation.

According to official reports, at approximately 1:15 p.m., a man fitting Oswald's description was seen talking with Dallas Patrolman J. D. Tippit near the intersection of 10th Street and Patton Avenue, about a mile from Oswald's rooming house. An argument ensued, the man was seen pulling a weapon from inside his waistband and firing several shots, hitting Tippit four times and killing him instantly with the last shot.

The frenzied assailant dashed past a movie ticket window and into the nearby Texas Theater on Jefferson Avenue. Acting on suspicion, the cashier and a local shoe store merchant called the Dallas Police. Within minutes, police had sealed off the theater, and turned on the lights in order to see the patrons. Following the cashier's description, police narrowed in on Oswald. Despite his attempted escape from the theater, he was apprehended and taken into custody.

Oswald was taken to Dallas police headquarters, booked, and interrogated. He denied having anything to do with the assassination of President Kennedy or the murder of Tippit. Oswald claimed he was having

Left to right:
Police used this photo to prove that Oswald owned a rifle, which he denied. Oswald claimed the photo was a fake • Sixth floor interior of the Texas School Book Depository • The Texas School Book Depository as seen from Dealey Plaza

Lee Harvey Oswald Assassinated

Left to right:
Oswald's jail transfer just seconds before Ruby pulls the trigger • Ruby assassinates Oswald in a hallway crowded with police officers and reporters • Jack Ruby

lunch at the time of the motorcade and had never met Officer Tippit. He even denied owning a rifle.

That afternoon, more than one hundred members of the press, radio, and television descended on Dallas Police Headquarters and camped out between Oswald's cell and the interrogation room, interviewing Oswald as he passed between the two rooms.

At 7:10 p.m. on November 22, Lee Harvey Oswald was formally charged with the murder of J.D. Tippit. The formal charge for the Kennedy

assassination was filed at 1:30 a.m. on Saturday, November 23.

Despite death threats, arrangements were made to move Oswald from the city jail to the Dallas County Jail. On Sunday morning, November 24, at 10:00 a.m., the press assembled in the basement of the city jail to cover the transfer. While ABC and CBS sent crews to film the event, NBC opted to cover the transfer in a live broadcast.

Surrounded by detectives, Oswald emerged from the basement jail office at approximately

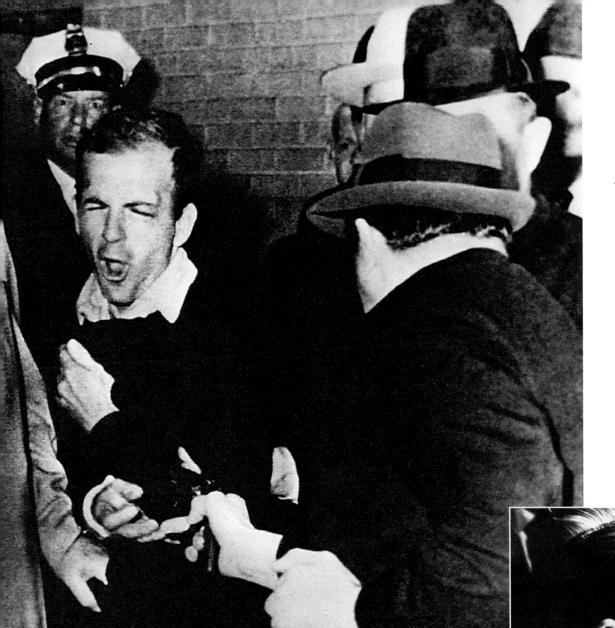

Oswald's murder became America's first see-it-as-it-happens national news event.

11:20 a.m. Just as WNEW radio newsman Ike Pappas began shouting questions to Oswald, a man leaped from the crowd of reporters, and in front of millions watching on television, pointed a .38-caliber revolver into Oswald's abdomen and shot him point-blank. Doubled over in pain, Oswald was rushed to Parkland Hospital and pronounced dead shortly after 1:00 p.m. Oswald's murder became America's first major see-it-as-it-happens national news event.

The man who killed Oswald was fifty-two-year-old Dallas nightclub owner Jack Ruby. Under interrogation, Ruby attributed his eye-for-an-eye murder of Oswald to depression and rage he was feeling over the President's assassination. On March 14, 1964, Ruby was found guilty of murder and sentenced to death. His sentence was later overturned. Ruby, still in custody, died of cancer in January 1967.

President Johnson *Declines Re-election Bid*

"If I've lost Cronkite, I've lost the American people."

March 31 1968

Lyndon Baines Johnson had become president through a cruel twist of fate, a man forced to replace a myth. Less than one year later, he was elected president on his own, defeating his Republican challenger Barry Goldwater in a landslide and declaring it "a mandate for unity." Capitalizing on his huge electoral triumph and a solidly Democratic-controlled Congress, President Johnson set about creating his "Great Society," signing into law the most sweeping program of social legislation since the days of Franklin Roosevelt.

Johnson expanded existing insurance benefits for the elderly by enacting the Medicare Social Security Bill. He created the Department of Housing and Urban Development, a Cabinet-level office responsible for administrating government-subsidized low-income housing. And, on August 6, 1965, President Johnson signed the Voting Rights Act which prohibited states from using tactics such as literacy tests and poll taxes to abate minority voter registration. Yet, Lyndon Baines Johnson remains best remembered as the president who presided over the darkest days of the Vietnam War, a conflict that tore apart generations, political parties, and finally, his own ability to govern.

U. S. involvement in Vietnam spanned the terms of five presidents, but the critical troop buildup followed the Gulf of Tonkin incident in August 1964, when North Vietnamese gunboats attacked a U.S. navy destroyer

in international waters. In response, Congress gave Johnson the authority to handle the conflict as he deemed necessary, without officially declaring war.

Within four years, U.S. troop levels rose to more than one-half million soldiers. But as the war widened, Americans watched its horrors unfold on television screens in their living rooms. U.S. and North Vietnamese death tolls became a fixture of the evening network newscasts. In early 1968, CBS newsman Walter Cronkite went to Vietnam to witness the war for himself. When he returned in March, he reported to the nation that the war did not appear to be either as noble in its aims, or as winnable in its practicable purpose, as its proponents had consistently claimed.

The effect on U.S. policy was immediate and profound. President Johnson watched Cronkite's report in despair. He reportedly turned from the television and told his aides, "If I've lost Cronkite, I've lost the American people."

A Gallup Poll gave Johnson only a thirty-five percent approval rating on his handling of the war. Johnson's own party was splitting at the seams.

Democratic Senators Eugene McCarthy and Robert Kennedy openly challenged Johnson for the presidential nomination. Johnson realized that, like Harry Truman before him, he'd allowed his administration to be crippled by an unpopular foreign war. On March 31, the networks pre-empted regular programming for President Johnson's televised speech on what was supposed to be the status of America's involvement in the war. Instead, Johnson revealed his own startling intentions.

Pointing at the mounting racial tensions and growing public denouncement of the country's involvement in the war, Johnson expressed concern for the "division in the American house," stating that he could not allow such divisions to permeate the presidency.

Then, pausing to stare into the camera, as if to make sure everyone was paying close attention, Johnson stunned the nation by announcing that he did not intend to run for re-election: "I shall not seek and I will not accept the nomination of my party as your president." Politicians and political pundits were caught completely off guard by Johnson's announcement. Reaction was mixed and debates waged on television and radio into the night.

The balance of Johnson's term in office saw one of the most violent eras in U.S. history. In April, civil rights leader Rev. Dr. Martin Luther King Jr. was assassinated, touching off riots in 125 cities across the nation. Two months later, Senator Robert Kennedy was gunned down in Los Angeles' Ambassador Hotel after having won the California Democratic Primary. In August, the whole world watched the streets of Chicago become blood-splattered and tear gas-filled as protesters clashed with police in demonstrations outside the Democratic National Convention. And the Vietnam War continued to escalate.

Lyndon Baines Johnson left the presidency in frustration. But the war, which had destroyed his relationship with the American people, would continue to bedevil his successors in that office for seven more years.

Top left to right:
Civil rights protest in Montgomery, Alabama, March 26, 1965 • Violence erupts between anti-Vietnam War protesters and police officers outside the Democratic National Convention in Chicago, 1968 • Protesters and police stand face to face at the Democratic Convention • Horrifying scenes of American involvement in Vietnam became fixtures of the evening network newscasts • A Poor People's demonstration and parade marched between the Lincoln and Washington Monuments, 1968
Below:
President Lyndon Baines Johnson

Martin Luther King Jr.
Assassinated

April 4
1968

Left to right:
Martin Luther King Jr. with wife Coretta and one of his young children • King delivers his famous "I Have a Dream" speech in a march on Washington, D.C. in 1963

From the pulpits to the streets of America's deep south, Reverend Dr. Martin Luther King Jr.'s voice was one heard above the din in the 1950s and 60s. America was struggling with its legacy of racial injustice, and King stood at the forefront of those attempting to mold a nation more equal and less separate.

Modeled on the philosophy of Indian pacifist Mahatma Gandhi, King pursued civil rights change through nonviolent resistance, principles for which he was awarded the Nobel Prize for Peace in 1964. He was an inspirational leader in the movement which resulted in passage of the Civil Rights Act of 1964 and the Voting Rights Act of 1965, landmark legislation allowing equal access to public accommodations and voting privileges for all.

In the hot summer months of 1963, King had his moment for which he may forever be best remembered. Speaking before a quarter of a million civil rights demonstrators in a march on the Washington, D.C., Capitol mall, he electrified the crowd with his "I Have a Dream" speech.

By 1968, though, Dr. King's leadership and his advocacy of peaceful resistance fell under constant attack from both inside and outside the movement. Militant factions challenged his relevancy as spokesman for the plight of African Americans, and the Federal Bureau of Investigation subjected him to constant harassment.

In March 1968, Dr. King accepted an invitation from striking sanitation workers in Memphis, Tennessee, to help them conduct a peaceful march. But despite King's presence, or because of it, the event turned violent, ending with several people beaten and one marcher killed. King returned to Memphis six days later, hoping to lead another, more peaceful protest.

He stood at the forefront of those attempting to mold a nation more equal and less separate.

Left to right:
James Earl Ray was
convicted of King's
murder. He died in
prison thirty years after
the assassination, still
proclaiming his
innocence • Mourners
decorate the balcony
in front of room 306 of
the Lorraine Motel
where King died

After his visit in March, a story in a local paper criticized King for having stayed at a white-owned hotel. When Dr. King and his entourage arrived in Memphis on April 3, they checked into the minority-owned Lorraine Motel instead.

Dr. King was scheduled to speak at the Mason Street Temple later that evening. That night, before a crowd of nearly two thousand, King delivered an impassioned speech in which he addressed the rumors of threats against his life. His words were courageous and confident, but they would soon become chillingly prophetic:

Well, I don't know what will happen now...Like anybody, I'd like to live a long life. Longevity has its place but I'm not concerned about that now. I just want to do God's will....So, I'm happy tonight. I'm not fearing any man. Mine eyes have seen the glory of the coming of the Lord.

King spent most of the next day indoors at the Lorraine Motel. Also in Memphis that day was a drifter with a long criminal record named James Earl Ray. The afternoon of April 4, Ray reportedly scoped the neighborhood of the Lorraine, having heard King was staying there. Driving his white 1966 Mustang, he realized that the rear windows of the rooming houses at 422 ½ South Main overlooked King's motel room. Ray parked his car and went in to get a room. Introducing himself as John Willard, Ray paid the $8.50 per week rent required for a room. He chose room 5 in the north wing, a room with a window that faced the balconies of the Lorraine Motel.

As King and his entourage prepared to leave that evening for dinner, Ray sat perched at the window of his floor's communal bathroom. Dr. King stepped onto the balcony in front of room 306 and spoke briefly with friends. Ray loaded a cartridge into his 30.06 Remington "Gamemaster" rifle, looked through the telescope sight, and took aim across the parking lot between the two buildings. Just over two hundred feet separated the rifle from its target.

At 6:01 p.m., a shot rang out in the courtyard. King was knocked back by a bullet that ripped through the right side of his jaw severing his spinal cord. Blood ran quickly from King's wound as his panicked associates desperately attempted to assist him. A group of police officers

"Like anybody, I'd like to live a long life... but I'm not concerned about that now. I just want to do God's will."

who happened to be at a fire station down the street arrived almost immediately and sought in vain for the killer.

Dr. King was rushed to Saint Joseph's Hospital where he was pronounced dead at 7:05 p.m.

Regularly scheduled broadcasts were interrupted with bulletins announcing the assassination, and televised evening news reports already in progress struggled to report what little information they had. Throughout the evening and the days that followed, the news also turned to cover the riots breaking out all across the country. King's assassination became an incendiary device within America's inner cities, and a nation watched its long-standing racial tensions explode.

King's aides had pointed police in the direction of the boarding house across from the Lorraine. Fingerprints found in room 5 and on the rifle, discarded just down the street from the boarding house, led investigators to James Earl Ray. He managed to elude the officials until June 8 when he was captured in London's Heathrow Airport. Ray confessed to the shooting but later recanted, claiming he was set up by a mysterious man named Raul, possibly an operative from the CIA, FBI, or U.S. military intelligence. His confession, though, was upheld and Ray was sentenced to life imprisonment where he died thirty years later, still proclaiming his innocence and seeking a new trial.

Above:
Supporters gather around King's family at the Southview Cemetery in Atlanta, Georgia

Robert Kennedy
Assassinated

1968

He spent much of his political career in the shadow of his older brother, but by the late 1960s, Robert F. Kennedy emerged as a symbol of dreams reborn. By 1968, he was not only the former U.S. Attorney General, but also the Democratic U.S. Senator from New York, and a candidate for the Democratic party's presidential nomination. His liberal agenda appealed to the young politically active generation, and the Kennedy name and good looks afforded him near rock star status among his constituency.

But not even a yearning for the Kennedy era reborn was powerful enough to secure the Democratic nomination, let alone the Oval Office. The campaign was grueling and the political landscape became even more treacherous on March 31, 1968.

In a speech to the nation, President Lyndon Johnson stunned the country and altered the political milieu by announcing he would not seek re-election in 1968. The Democratic nomination was up for grabs and Kennedy found himself in a three-way race with Vice President Hubert Humphrey and Senator Eugene McCarthy.

Following his defeat in the Oregon primary, Kennedy strategists began concentrating on the crucial June 4 California primary. As his campaign continued, it began gaining a distinctively

After his brother's assassination, Robert became the natural inheritor of the Kennedy mantle.

positive momentum. Although the crowds of supporters seemed to grow at every stop, the campaign was also plagued by constant death threats; Kennedy was even hit by a rock during a motorcade appearance.

Robert Kennedy's candidacy hit its stride in California, and by late evening on June 4, he appeared to have won its primary. With the nomination nearing his grasp, Kennedy's victory speech at the Ambassador Hotel in Los Angeles was exuberant. After generously sharing the credit for the win, he triumphantly declared, "It's on to Chicago" and the Democratic nomination.

Before heading back to his suite to celebrate the victory, Kennedy was to hold a press conference in the hotel's Colonial Room, which had been turned into a makeshift pressroom. In order to avoid the crowds, Kennedy and his family, supporters, and bodyguards were guided through the kitchen. The Ambassador Hotel's maitre d' Carl Uecker and a private security guard named Thane Cesar escorted them through the narrow passageway. Kennedy's entourage included his wife Ethel, Olympic champion Rafer Johnson, Los Angeles Rams lineman Roosevelt Grier, a cameraman for ABC TV, and a reporter named Andrew West from KRKD-AM, the Los Angeles affiliate of the Mutual Broadcasting System.

Realizing the opportunity for an exclusive interview, West turned on his tape recorder and began interviewing the Senator as they made their way to the Colonial Room. Suddenly, a Jordanian

Clockwise from left: Robert F. Kennedy as Attorney General • Kennedy on the presidential campaign trail, 1968 • Robert Kennedy (middle) with brothers John (left) and Edward (right) in Hyannisport, Massachusetts, July 1960

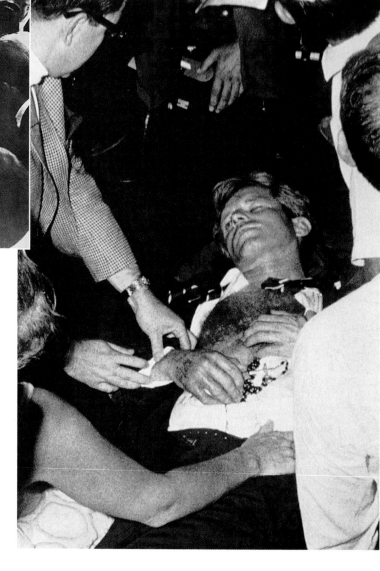

"He still has the gun.
The gun is pointed at me....
Get his thumb and break
it if you have to!"

Left to right:
The chaos surrounding
Robert Kennedy just
moments after he was
shot. His wife Ethel,
wearing the white dress,
looks on • Robert
Kennedy lies mortally
wounded on the floor of
the Ambassador Hotel,
Los Angeles

man named Sirhan Sirhan lunged out of the crowd, aiming a .22-caliber pistol, and firing it repeatedly at Kennedy. Uecker attempted to restrain the assailant and was joined by Johnson who grabbed the gunman's hand. But Sirhan continued to struggle, waving the gun wildly, and at one point aiming it directly at West. West began shouting, "Get the gun, get the gun," and even instructed a bodyguard to "break his thumbs if you have to, just get the gun." Finally, Kennedy's guards tackled Sirhan to the floor.

The kitchen area was in chaos. The senator lay bleeding to death on the floor, five others were wounded, and Kennedy's aides struggled with his assailant. In the midst of it all, a kitchen employee named Juan Romero tried to comfort the dying Senator, placing a rosary into his hand. Kennedy whispered to Romero, "Is everyone all right?"

Campaign workers once jubilant were now dazed by the shock. Pleas for "a doctor in the house" echoed repeatedly from the podium from which Kennedy had spoken only a few moments before.

Within minutes, Robert Kennedy was rushed to a nearby trauma center, then to a local hospital, where he died in the early morning hours of June 6, with his wife, sister-in-law Jacqueline,

Sirhan kept his identity a secret until his brothers saw his face in a newspaper and notified police.

and other friends and relatives at his side. Robert Francis Kennedy was forty-two years old.

Kennedy was buried at Arlington National Cemetery next to his brother. The live television and radio coverage of the services repeated the drama of his brother's funeral just five years earlier.

Sirhan kept his identity a secret until his brothers were astonished to see his face in a newspaper and notified police. The twenty-four-year-old immigrant was reportedly angry at Kennedy's strong support of Israel's military policy. Sirhan Bishara Sirhan was found guilty of first-degree murder and sentenced to death. His sentence later was commuted to life imprisonment.

Media coverage of presidential candidates has evolved due in large part to the Kennedy assassination. Only radio reporter Andrew West and an ABC television cameraman walked with Kennedy through the kitchen area at the Ambassador Hotel that night. In contrast, 1984 presidential candidate Reverend Jesse Jackson had two crews from each of the television networks with him at all times. One crew was assigned to cover the scheduled campaign events, while the second team, dubbed "the body watch crew," was assigned to follow his every move. Such massive media attention keeps both would-be assassins and fans alike away from popular political figures.

Left to right:
Kennedy assassin Sirhan B. Sirhan as he leaves jail-house courtroom hearings, June 28, 1968 •
Robert Kennedy's family follows his coffin down the steps of St. Patrick's Cathedral, New York City, June 9, 1968. Kennedy is buried in Arlington National Cemetery

Apollo 11
Man Walks on Moon

July 20
1969

I believe that this nation should commit itself to achieving the goal before this decade is out, of landing a man on the moon and returning him safely to earth.

—President John F. Kennedy

With these words spoken early in his term as president in 1961, John F. Kennedy gave eloquent voice to the challenge of looking beyond an arms race with the Soviet Union to a more tangible but peaceful quest, with glory as the prize. On July 16, 1969, at 9:32 a.m. eastern daylight time, three American astronauts courageously climbed atop a 363-foot-high *Saturn V* rocket and blasted into space to claim that prize for the United States.

Shortly after their textbook launch from Cape Kennedy, Florida, Commander Neil Armstrong, USAF Colonel Edwin Aldrin Jr., and USAF Lieutenant Colonel Michael Collins settled into

"There's a foot on the moon! Wow! Oh boy! Hot diggity dog! Yes sir!"

Earth's orbit for a final instrument check and to set their spacecraft on a course for the moon, a journey that would take them more than two hundred forty thousand miles from home.

Throughout their trip, the astronauts transmitted televised greetings to those back on Earth. Millions of curious television viewers watched the men carry out various tests and experiments. Armstrong, Aldrin, and Collins also got a chance to share their feelings with the world. Armstrong described his view of the moon's surface, "It looks very much like the pictures but, like the difference between watching a real football game and one on TV, there's no substitute for actually being here."

Four days into the flight, *Apollo 11* fired its propulsion system, easing the spacecraft into orbit approximately sixty-five miles above the moon's surface. Armstrong and Aldrin climbed through the pressurized crawlway that connected the *Columbia* command module to the lunar lander, called the *Eagle*. After powering up the *Eagle*, the two astronauts radioed to Houston that "the *Eagle* has wings." Armstrong and Aldrin undocked the lunar module, leaving Collins behind in the capsule, and began descending to the surface of the moon at a rate of two hundred feet per second. Although the *Eagle* was carrying just two American astronauts, millions on Earth journeyed with them by television.

With just minutes of fuel remaining, the astronauts realized they were four miles away from their predetermined landing spot at the relatively smooth Sea of Tranquility. Faced with a rocky surface far too hostile to permit a smooth landing, Armstrong overrode the computer control and manually glided the *Eagle* over the moon's surface to a safer landing area. Watching on television, the world held its breath as it listened to the live broadcast of Aldrin coaching Armstrong to the surface, "Looking good, down a half…Thirty feet, down two and a half…Kicking up some dust…Drifting to the right…OK. Engine stop!" It was a heart-stopping exhibition of skill and courage, and mission control breathed a collective sigh of relief when Armstrong shut off the engine and reported, "Houston, Tranquility base here. The *Eagle* has landed." It was 4:17:43 p.m., July 20, 1969.

Six and one-half hours later, Armstrong and Aldrin were suited up and ready to open the hatch. As Armstrong slowly climbed down the nine-rung ladder, he released a television camera that would include the world in his descent.

*Left to right:
Apollo 11 blasts off,
July 16, 1969 • Astronauts
Neil Armstrong, Michael
Collins, and Edwin "Buzz"
Aldrin Jr. • Houston,
Texas-based
mission control*

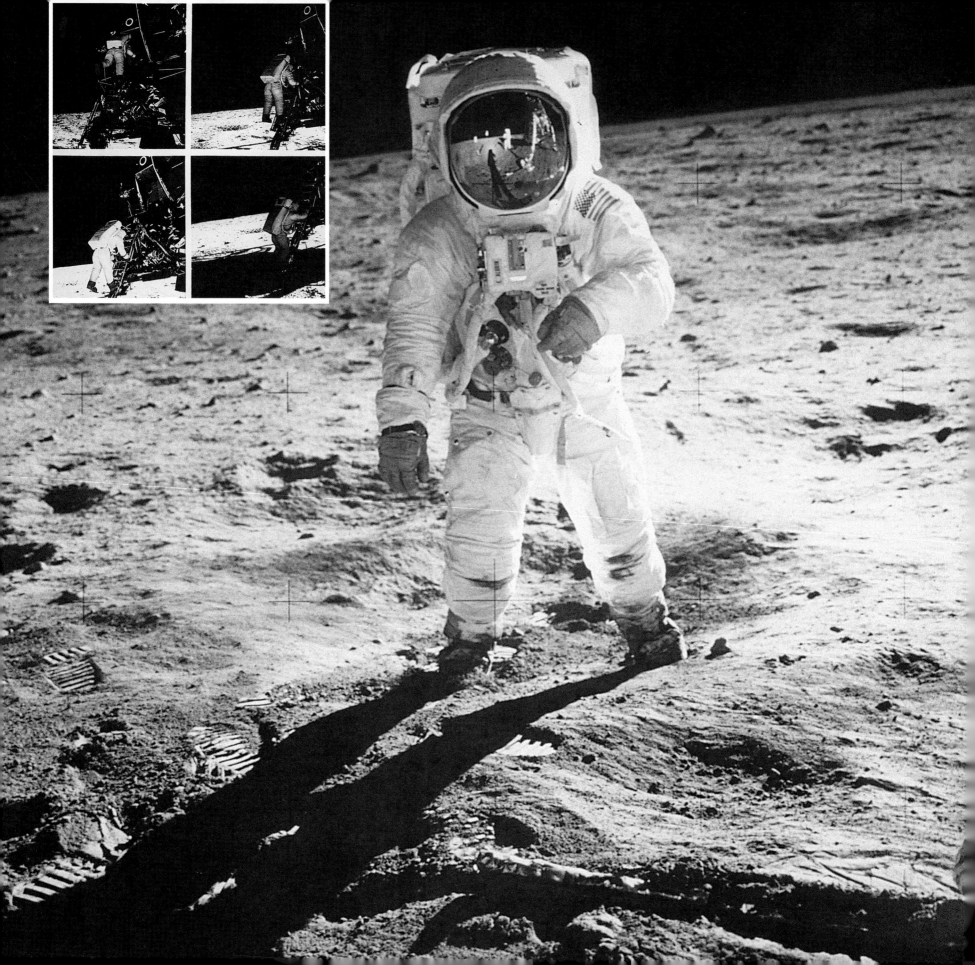

Apollo 13 was in serious trouble. It was two hundred thousand miles from Earth on a course that would take it to lunar orbit rather than home. There had been an explosion and the extent of the damage was as yet unknown. The main oxygen supply was gone. The fuel cells that supplied power and water depended on that oxygen. Without power, the command module would be completely inert, without air, light, heat, communications, or any ability to navigate. The cooling system necessary to keep on-board electronic systems at safe operating temperatures in a weightless environment used the water made by the fuel cells. If the cooling system failed, the on-board computers and control systems would go down one-by-one and *Apollo 13* would effectively shut down. The command module's batteries would only power it for ten hours, a reserve intended only for final approach and re-entry.

The first step was to shut down the command module and take refuge in the lunar module. The lunar module had been intended to support two people for a little over two days but, by shutting down all non-essential systems, three could live in it for about eighty-four hours. *Apollo 13* had to be put on a course that would return it home before power and water reserves were exhausted. The only propulsion system available was the one aboard the lunar module. The lunar module's rocket engines were designed to take it down to the moon's surface from orbit and bring it up again. It had never been intended to provide thrust for the much larger *Apollo* spacecraft. Even if the lunar module's engines were up to the job, the

Left to right:
An entire panel on the service module was blown away by the explosion on an oxygen tank. Two of the three fuel cells are visible just above the heavily damaged area • Flight directors cheer the successful splashdown of *Apollo 13*

"Houston, we've had a problem."

usual procedures for doing mid-course corrections were not practical with the command module shut down. An alternative procedure would have to be devised that did not rely on command module systems.

The immediate need was to alter course so that *Apollo 13* would swing around the moon and head back to Earth rather than enter lunar orbit. After extensive calculations, mission control ordered a thirty-five-second burn of the lunar module engines five hours after the explosion. *Apollo 13* was now on a course that would return it to Earth, but on its present trajectory it would arrive with practically no reserves of power or water.

Mission control discovered that it would be possible to reduce *Apollo 13*'s travel time by almost ten hours, but it would require substantial additional use of the lunar module's engines. The engineers who had designed the lunar module's propulsion system were consulted and confirmed that the lunar module had adequate capacity for the proposed burn. Meanwhile, the crew of *Apollo 13* was engaged in the intricate job of ensuring that the spacecraft was correctly aligned. Alignment was usually done with a computerized version of the old naval sextant. Because a cloud of debris from the explosion surrounded *Apollo 13*, it was not possible to use a star sighting, so the sun was used as an alignment star. Two hours after *Apollo 13* rounded the moon, the lunar module's engines were fired for five minutes and *Apollo 13* was on the way to a mid-Pacific splashdown.

Mission control and the *Apollo* contractors turned their attention to the complicated business of creating a new mission plan for the return home. A detailed timeline had to be established that ensured that necessary course corrections,

Apollo 13 was heading home, but the trip was not a comfortable one.

maneuvers, and command module power-up were done in a way that used as little power and water coolant as possible. Many of these maneuvers were novel. Mission planners had never needed to consider the consequences of separating the service module from the linked command module and lunar module or separating the command module and the lunar module only an hour or so before re-entry. Teams of experts explored these issues and hundreds of others for most of *Apollo 13*'s return trip, finishing in three days a job that usually requires three months.

Apollo 13 was heading home, but the trip was not a comfortable one. Because of the critical shortage of water, each crew member was allowed only six ounces a day. Between dehydration and an understandable lack of interest in food, *Apollo 13* astronauts lost more weight than the crew of any other mission. They were also cold. *Apollo 13* was stuffed with heat-producing electronic equipment that by itself kept the cabin at shirt-sleeve temperatures. With most systems powered off, temperatures dropped to as low as 38 degrees Fahrenheit

and most surfaces were covered with condensation. Sleep or even useful rest is difficult at such temperatures and the crew's fatigue was becoming obvious. The lunar module's equipment for removing carbon dioxide was overloaded and the crew worked with mission control to make an impromptu repair.

An hour before re-entry, the lunar module, which had been their lifeboat, was discarded. Mission control bid, "Farewell *Aquarius*, and we thank you." Lovell's benediction was: "She was a good ship."

Clear of the lunar module, command module *Odyssey* followed its course to a precise landing, splashing down just three and one-half miles from the recovery ship, the carrier *Iwo Jima*, after a harrowing mission of 142 hours and fifty-four minutes.

Apollo 13 was followed by four further *Apollo* missions, all with successful and scientifically fruitful lunar landings. The last *Apollo* astronaut stepped off the moon on December 14, 1972. No one has announced plans to return.

Left to right: Recovery helicopters transport the astronauts to the USS *Iwo Jima* while frogmen are left to handle the spacecraft *Odyssey* • The *Odyssey* shortly after splashdown • *Apollo 13* astronauts (left to right) Fred Haise Jr., James Lovell, and Jack Swigert

Kent State
Massacre

Left to right:
The body of a slain victim lies on the campus of Kent State • Kent students run for cover as Ohio National Guardsmen fire upon them • Students toss tear gas canisters back at National Guardsmen

Until May 4, 1970, Kent State was an average Middle American university. The northeastern Ohio school of approximately twenty-one thousand people drew the majority of its student body from nearby, working-class towns. Though the school experienced an average amount of dissent and protest over U.S. participation in Vietnam in the spring of 1969, the 1969-1970 school year was a relatively quiet one. Until May 1970, Kent State's largest turmoil of that year stemmed from the school's annual mudfight.

President Richard Nixon's April 30 speech ended Kent's peace. Students met on the afternoon of Friday, May 1, protesting Nixon's pledge to send American troops to Cambodia in support of the South Vietnamese presence there. At that time, they planned another demonstration for the following Monday.

That evening, warm spring temperatures drew locals and students into the downtown bar district. Crowds outside the bars grew and became unruly. Kent Mayor Leroy Satrom's attempt to thwart destruction in the downtown by declaring a state of emergency failed. His orders to close the bars and clear the area only forced more people into the streets, where police, students, and locals alike dodged flying beer bottles, broken glass, and tear gas canisters. Police finally herded the crowd toward the university campus. By the end of the night, vandals had caused thousands of dollars in damage, breaking windows and trashing storefronts. Satrom called the Ohio governor for assistance and received assurance that a National Guard officer would be dispatched to observe Kent activities.

The following morning, rumors of radical activities were rampant on the KSU campus.

When the smoke cleared, four students had been killed and nine wounded.

Mayor Satrom took no chances, imposing a dusk-to-dawn curfew on the city, and ordering students restricted to the campus. He then alerted the Ohio National Guard.

Despite the precautions, by the evening of May 2 people gathered in the Commons, chanting anti-war slogans and listening to fiery rhetoric. The crowd, more than one thousand strong, marched to the ROTC building and set it on fire. Firemen arrived on the scene only to abandon their efforts when the crowd attacked them and slashed their hoses. By midnight, the National Guard, armed with tear gas and bayonets, cleared the campus, forcing students and bystanders into dormitories and other campus buildings, where many spent the night.

In response to the escalating violence, Governor James A. Rhodes arrived on the university's campus the next morning. His press

Below:
The Ohio National
Guard killed four students
on their own campus.
None of the four were
confirmed protesters

conference vow to "use every weapon possible to eradicate the problem," led some school administrators and National Guardsmen to believe that martial law was declared. In fact, such a decree—in part banning rallies and public gatherings—never had been issued.

The day gave way to a night of violence as students and guardsmen clashed once again. Helicopters hovering overhead fired tear gas on students below. As protesters attempted to escape, some were bayoneted and clubbed. Students were again pursued and prodded back to their dormitories.

The demonstration scheduled for Monday, May 4 began as planned. As classes broke for the noon hour, students filled the Commons area, some to protest, some to satisfy their curiosity, and some merely to eat lunch. National Guardsmen, still believing that martial law was in effect, attempted to disperse the crowd but were met with hostile chants and thrown rocks.

Dressed in riot gear and carrying M-1 rifles, more than one hundred members of the National Guard pushed the crowd out of the Commons area and into a practice athletic field. The guard realized, however, that it had fenced

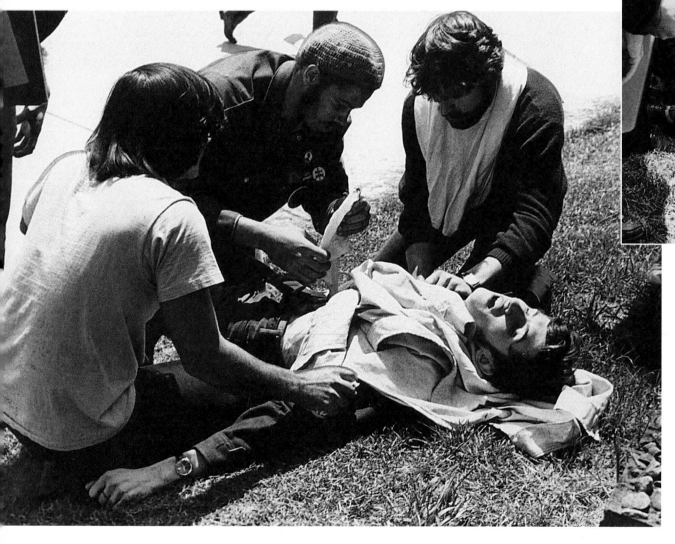

*A special grand jury
placed ultimate blame
on Kent State's administration.
The National Guard
escaped official accountability.*

itself in and moved to retrace its steps. As the guard moved up the crest of Bunker Hill and away from the practice field, twenty-eight guardsmen turned to face the students and fired sixty-one bullets into the crowd. With its thirteen seconds of gunfire, the guard killed four students and wounded nine, one of whom became permanently paralyzed. Director of Radio-TV Information for Kent State University John Preston Smith was on campus at the time of the shooting and provided an eyewitness account. The national media broadcast bulletins of the rioting and shooting deaths of the students.

That afternoon, a county court judge legally closed Kent State. The university re-opened for its summer session as investigations into the event continued. Despite a Justice Department Summary of the FBI's probe into the incident that stated that the shooting was "not proper and not in order," the Special Grand Jury of Portage County placed ultimate blame on Kent State's administration for not being able to rid the campus of protesters. Twenty-five students and professors were indicted by the Grand Jury while individual guardsmen and the guard as a whole escaped official accountability and blame.

Left to right:
Kent State students demonstrate their treatment in Washington, D.C. • Hundreds of mourners and student supporters attend the funeral of Jeffrey Miller, a victim of the National Guard assault

Munich Olympics
Tragedy

1972

Above:
Israeli wrestlers Zeev
Friedman, David Berger,
and Joseph Romano were
three of the eleven
athletes slain by Arab
terrorists. Coach Tuvia
Sokolovsky (far right)
was one of two team
members who escaped

Violent clashes of political and religious ideologies are a disturbing reality of our world, but for a few short weeks every four years, the summer Olympic Games are an island of peace amid a sea of conflict. On September 5, 1972, the Olympic ideal was dashed when the Games of the XX Olympiad in Munich, Germany, became the site of the most violent act of politically motivated terrorism in Olympic history.

Twelve thousand visiting athletes and staff were housed in Munich's Olympic Village. Every precaution of the time had been taken to protect those living within the heavily guarded compound. However, despite the security measures, eight armed terrorists managed to infiltrate the Village in the early morning hours of September 5.

Their target was the apartment complex housing the Israeli national contingent. The terrorists stormed into two apartments, and into the lives of thirteen members of the Israeli team.

In the chaos that followed, two team members successfully escaped while two others were shot dead as they tried to run. The remaining nine became the terrorists' pawns.

The commandos identified themselves as the Black September organization and immediately made their demands: the lives of their hostages in exchange for the freedom of 236 Arab prisoners held in Israel, plus air transportation to fly them and their captives to an unspecified location. If their conditions were not met by 9 a.m., they would begin killing their hostages.

The focus of the international media had switched from the athletic competitions to the bloody siege in the Village compound. Images of the hooded terrorists on the balcony of the seized apartment building were flashed around the globe, and the world watched as the standoff intensified.

The terrorists stormed into two apartments, and into the lives of thirteen members of the Israeli team.

Authorities surrounded the block, but heeded the terrorists' promise to begin killing hostages if a rescue was attempted. Negotiations gained little movement toward either the release of the hostages or the fulfillment of the terrorists' demands and the deadline was extended six times, the last one set at 9 p.m.

The terrorists were presented two alternative offers in exchange for the release of their hostages: they could be paid a large ransom and given safe passage out of Germany, or West German officials would take the place of the Israeli athletes as hostages.

The Black September group rejected both offers, instead naming their destination as Cairo, Egypt. They demanded that by the time they landed in Cairo, the Arab prisoners would be released and waiting for them at the airport.

The Olympic task force acceded to the terrorists' request for transportation. At 10 p.m. the commandos and the Israeli captives were transported to two helicopters and flown to a military airfield where they would presumably make their escape. Upon their arrival, the crisis that appeared to be nearing an end took a violent turn when German police launched a surprise

Left to right:
Terrorists identifying themselves as Black September occupied two apartments of this building in the Olympic Village • A terrorist peers over the balcony of an Israeli apartment • A German policeman surveys the area above the block where terrorists hold the Israeli hostages

attack in a desperate attempt to liberate the hostages.

A ninety-minute standoff ensued, with police marksmen and the terrorists embroiled in a continuous gun battle. It ended in tragedy when one terrorist threw a live grenade into one of the helicopters, killing all five hostages inside, while the other terrorists shot and killed the remaining hostages. When the smoke cleared, the results were horrific: one German police officer, five terrorists, and all nine Israeli athletes were killed. Three terrorists were captured.

The world awoke shocked by the news, particularly since many had gone to bed following an erroneous broadcast interruption reporting that the hostages had been freed after a late-night gun battle. Israel and the world had celebrated the false reports at the time and settled in for the night. But the jubilation felt that night would only intensify the pain experienced the next morning.

Despite the protests of many, the International Olympic Committee concluded that ending the Games would mean a victory for terrorism, and that the Games must go on. On September 6, a memorial was held at Olympic Stadium and was attended by a capacity crowd of eighty thousand, while millions more around the world watched via television. The Olympic Games solemnly continued the next day.

The events that unfolded on September 5, in front of a worldwide viewing audience, have had a lasting effect on the staging of future Olympic Games. As a result, Olympic officials increased their already heavy and high-tech security measures, and subsequent Games went off without major incident until those hosted by Atlanta in 1996.

Left to right:
Numbers mark the areas where bullets pierced a helicopter in the shootout • Wreckage of a helicopter that held five Israeli hostages. A terrorist threw a hand grenade into the helicopter, killing all on board • Family members of the slain athletes grieve as coffins arrive at Tel Aviv Airport • Flags stand at half-mast in Olympic Stadium • Mourners attend a memorial service in Olympic Stadium

Nixon *Resigns*

August 8
1974

The career of Richard Nixon was one of the most volatile in the history of twentieth century politics. As a newly elected Republican member of the House, Nixon achieved political celebrity in 1948 by leading the attack against Alger Hiss, a State Department diplomat who had been accused of leaking sensitive papers to the Soviet Union. Nixon successfully parlayed his new fame into a Senate seat in 1950. In 1952 he was selected as Dwight D. Eisenhower's running mate and served as vice president for two terms. A narrow loss to JFK in the 1960 presidential election, followed in 1962 by an unsuccessful bid for California governor, left his political future in doubt.

In 1968, the Democratic party was in turmoil. Lyndon Johnson declined to run for re-election, and an assassin's bullet killed lead candidate Robert Kennedy. The Democrats hosted a chaotic convention later that summer in Chicago, during which protesters and police clashed in the streets. Ultimately, the events that year aided the demise of the Democratic party and, again by the slimmest of margins, Richard Nixon's political career was resurrected, this time as president of the United States.

In his first term as president, Nixon inherited what Johnson characterized as "divisions in the American house" and vowed to begin bringing the country together, attempting to untangle U.S. involvement in Vietnam and Southeast Asia. In February 1972, reversing nearly twenty years of American policy, Richard Nixon opened the diplomatic door to the People's Republic of China and became the first U.S. president ever to visit the communist nation. In June, Nixon became the first U.S. president to visit Moscow where he signed an arms treaty with Soviet Communist Party Chairman Leonid Brezhnev.

The Watergate complex break-in was seen as a "blatantact of political espionage."

In November 1972, Richard Nixon was re-elected president by the widest percentage ever amassed by a Republican, resembling the landslide victories of Democratic presidents Franklin Roosevelt and Lyndon Johnson. But within six months, Nixon's incredible victory would be tainted by allegations of improprieties and cover-ups.

The June 1972 break-in at Democratic National Committee offices in the Watergate building was seen as a "blatant act of political espionage" by Democratic Committee Chairman, Lawrence F. O'Brien. The burglars were identified as a group of anti-Castro Cuban exiles and James McCord, a former CIA agent and security coordinator for the Committee to Re-elect the President. Their trail led to E. Howard Hunt, a CIA-retiree who worked as a White House consultant, and G. Gordon Liddy, legal consul for Nixon's re-election committee.

Clockwise from left:
The infamous Watergate Hotel • Anti-Nixon rally in New York City, November 10, 1973 • Nixon flashes the "Victory" sign at the 1968 GOP National Convention

Left with no alternatives, Nixon reluctantly handed over the tapes, including the "smoking gun."

Left to right:
North Carolina Senator Sam Ervin (second from left) led the televised Senate committee hearings • White House aide H.R. Haldeman testifies before the Senate committee • Nixon says goodbye to the White House staff, August 9, 1974 • Vice President Gerald Ford takes the oath of office from Chief Justice Warren Burger, August 9, 1974

In January 1973, Federal Judge John Sirica sentenced the four burglars and Hunt to extensive prison terms. McCord plea-bargained by proclaiming the involvement of three top Nixon officials: Attorney General John Mitchell; Mitchell's deputy, Jeb Magruder; and White House counsel John Dean. Nixon continued to deny any wrongdoing and instead announced that he was ordering a new investigation. Two federal grand juries and the press also were investigating.

The term "Watergate" began to apply to myriad misdeeds, all of which the U.S. Congress decided to investigate with a select committee headed by North Carolina Senator Sam Ervin. On April 30, 1973, Nixon announced that his two chief White House aides, H.R. Haldeman and John Ehrlichman, were resigning, as were Attorney General Richard Kleindienst, who succeeded Mitchell, and White House attorney John Dean. Acceding to the demands of a Senate resolution, the new Attorney General, Elliot Richardson, named Archibald Cox as a Special Prosecutor on May 18. Cox was given broad powers to investigate criminal activity associated with the 1972 campaign.

Dean took the stand in front of the Ervin Committee in June and testified that Nixon himself had been lying, and that he had known about the White House cover-up attempts since at least September 1972. In July, Alexander Butterfield, a former aide to Haldeman, told the committee that Nixon had installed voice-activated recorders and taped all his White House conversations.

Cox subpoenaed nine of the tapes and, despite executive privilege arguments, the courts supported his demands. Nixon was still unwilling to surrender the tapes and ordered Attorney General Richardson to fire Cox. Richardson refused and resigned. William Ruchelshaus, Richardson's second in command, was also ordered to fire Cox, but he also refused to do so and resigned. Finally, Robert Bork, the Solicitor General, agreed to do the President's bidding. The press made much of this "Saturday Night Massacre" and under intense pressure another Special Prosecutor, Leon Jaworski, was appointed.

"I must put the interests of America first....Therefore, I shall resign the presidency effective at noon tomorrow."

Jaworski also demanded the White House surrender the tapes and eventually won a Supreme Court order commanding the President to do so.

Left with no alternatives, Nixon reluctantly handed over the tapes, including the "smoking gun," a recorded conversation between Nixon and Haldeman on June 23, 1972, a time when Nixon had long asserted that he knew nothing about the break-in that occurred just six days earlier. The two men are heard discussing Mitchell's involvement, ordering a cover-up, and planning to use the CIA for protection.

Throughout, the House Judiciary Committee had been holding hearings on impeachment. It decided to recommend impeaching Nixon on three counts: obstruction of justice, abuse of presidential powers, and defiance of the committee's subpoenas. The recommendation was sent to the floor of the House of Representatives.

Hopelessly snarled in Watergate and prodded by the threat of impeachment, Nixon went before the American people one last time. On August 8, 1974, speaking on radio and television from the Oval Office, Nixon announced that he "must put the interests of America first.... Therefore, I shall resign the presidency effective at noon tomorrow."

The next day, Vice President Gerald R. Ford took the oath of office to become the thirty-eighth president of the United States, declaring, "Our long national nightmare is over."

Through his resignation, Nixon removed himself from the threat of impeachment, but not from possible criminal charges. As hard as President Ford tried to focus on the country's business, he continued to be dogged by Watergate.

In an astonishing move just one month after Nixon announced his resignation, Ford offered Nixon an unconditional pardon for all crimes he may have committed in the White House.

Nixon accepted the pardon. But the "tranquillity" Ford hoped to maintain through the gesture erupted with venomous criticism that lasted throughout his term, and swept Jimmy Carter into office on a mandate for change.

Saigon *Falls*

April 30
1975

Left to right:
The International
Conference on Vietnam
began shortly after the
United States and North
and South Vietnam signed
a peace treaty • Americans
leave a helicopter that
had carried them from
Vietnam. The U.S.
evacuated more than
seven thousand people
before Saigon fell

In late 1972, the governments of the United States and North Vietnam were engaged in on-again, off-again, cease-fire negotiations. Yet, despite the promising assertion on October 26 from National Security Adviser Henry Kissinger that negotiations between the two governments were continuing and that "peace was at hand," the U.S. military soon resumed devastating and costly bombing raids.

Finally, on January 27, 1973, in Paris, France, the governments of the United States and North and South Vietnam signed a long-anticipated peace treaty. It called for an immediate cease-fire, the withdrawal of American troops from South Vietnam, the return of American prisoners of war from North Vietnam, and the creation of an international military force to supervise the truce.

American forces made a slow, final withdrawal from South Vietnam; a process President Richard Nixon called "peace with honor." It was

a dubiously anticlimactic end to America's combat role in the Vietnam War which had claimed more than fifty-eight thousand American lives. Once U.S. troops were sent home, the North Vietnamese guilefully assumed an impertinent and aggressive stance against the South and fragile peace accords began to crumble.

Meanwhile, war-weary America focused on healing itself of the trauma caused by years of divisiveness over Vietnam. But no sooner had the mending process begun than the country was subjected to yet another national nightmare: Watergate. After no end of revelations of cover-ups and payoffs that led congressional investigators all the way to the Oval Office, on August 8, 1974, Nixon resigned.

The final withdrawal of U.S. troops and personnel from South Vietnam was left to Nixon's successor, Gerald Ford. But as the peace accords unraveled, and stability in South Vietnam

The U.S. enacted the largest emergency evacuation of the war, removing thousands of Vietnamese from their war-torn country.

continued to erode, the administration accelerated the evacuation process in early 1975.

With the Vietcong closing in on Saigon, the U.S. mission enacted the largest emergency helicopter evacuation of the war, removing thousands of willing Vietnamese citizens from their war-torn country in the last days of April. When news of the shelling of nearby Tan Son Nhut airport reached the capital city, panic reigned. Thousands of Vietnamese fearing communist rule sought refuge within the walls of the American embassy.

For eighteen hours, one by one, U.S. military helicopters, dodging relentless sniper fire, landed on the roof of the embassy just long enough to ferry a few more fortunate passengers to aircraft carriers waiting offshore.

On April 30, 1975, as communist forces amassed on the outskirts of Saigon, President Ford,

Top to bottom:
U.S. Marines rush to evacuate the last remaining Americans in Saigon, April 29, 1975 • In a desperate attempt to escape their country, Vietnam citizens hang on the back of a Chinook helicopter as it takes off

Left to right:
An American official punches a refugee in the face as he tries to board an already overloaded evacuation helicopter • Evacuees line up to be taken from the American embassy in Saigon to Navy ships waiting off the coast • A bus carrying evacuees is swarmed by Vietnamese citizens outside the American embassy, April 29, 1975

who was monitoring the situation with his advisors in the private quarters of the White House, ordered Ambassador Graham Martin and the remaining personnel to leave immediately. Prolonging the evacuation process further could cost even more American lives. So, despite promises of safe passage, some four hundred Vietnamese loyalists desperately waiting their turn on the embassy grounds were to be left behind.

To avoid hysteria, a plan was devised to systematically pull the Marine guards from their posts at the embassy walls and into the building. When the signal was given, the soldiers calmly made their way into the embassy. When the loyalists on the embassy grounds and the angry crowd outside the embassy walls realized what was happening, the scene turned chaotic.

The Marine guards cut power to the building's two elevators, and the remaining personnel climbed the stairwell, closing and locking the gates behind them to keep the mob at bay. The last American staff members and soldiers on duty gathered on the roof of the building, and in groups of twenty, boarded helicopters and were transported away.

The Vietnam War was the first war with almost instantaneous television coverage, and the fall of Saigon was its finale. For as long as they could, the remaining television and radio journalists beamed back to America the sights and sounds of the North Vietnamese army as its tanks rolled into the city. After twenty years, American involvement in a war that had never been officially declared was finally over.

Despite promises of safe passage, some four hundred loyalists were left behind.

Elvis *Dies*

August 16
1977

Above:
Elvis circa 1950s

For most of his life, Elvis Presley personified the "American dream." The dirt-poor country boy, nurtured on a cultural cuisine of gospel and rhythm and blues, created a sound of his own that would irreversibly change the course of popular music and make him a star of colossal proportion. For twenty years, Elvis Presley sold more records, received more accolades, and performed to more sold-out arenas than any other entertainer in history. His career included thirty-three movies and 105 Top 40 hits.

By the time Elvis' first hit, "Heartbreak Hotel," had entered the charts in 1956, he was well on his way to fame. With the help of his agent, Colonel Tom Parker, Elvis toured relentlessly, spending more time in transit from concert to concert than he did on stage. He appeared, much to the chagrin of *Ozzie and Harriet*-era parents, as sex with a voice, using his style of dress, lyrics, and gyrations to seduce audiences.

Hearts did indeed break in 1958 when a twenty-four-year-old Elvis met the girl of his dreams, Priscilla Beaulieu, while serving as an army gun tanker in West Germany. Ten years his junior, Priscilla idolized the man who would one day be her husband. After Elvis' years in the military, he returned to Graceland, his Memphis, Tennessee, estate, and married Priscilla in 1967.

Their marriage, however, would not last long. Priscilla gave birth to a daughter, Lisa Marie, less than a year after their wedding day, and Elvis grew distant from his wife shortly thereafter. The couple divorced in 1972.

As Elvis' marriage ended, so did his string of twenty No. 1 hits—the last being "Suspicious Minds" in 1969. Still, Elvis continued to sell out every venue, further securing his place in American history.

His fame stretched all the way into the White House, where he appeared unannounced

in late December 1970 requesting a visit with President Richard Nixon. Nixon obliged, and the "King" entered the Oval Office clad in a crushed purple velvet suit and gargantuan gold belt. At Elvis' request, Nixon designated him a "special assistant" in the Federal Bureau of Narcotics and Dangerous Drugs—a deep irony given that prescription drug use eventually would contribute to Elvis' death.

By mid-1977, at the age of forty-two, Elvis's life was a numbing cycle of concert touring followed by drug-induced, reclusive hibernation. When he eventually ventured from his second-floor bedroom suite, Elvis spent his final week seeing hometown friends and relatives, playing racquetball, reading, and talking of the upcoming tour that was to start August 17 before

Clockwise from left:
Elvis' Memphis mansion, Graceland • To his 1950s audiences, Elvis was sex with a voice • Though Elvis had his last No. 1 hit in 1969, his popularity grew throughout the 1970s, mostly due to his flashy concert demeanor

"Flash—The King of Rock-n-Roll is dead."

a sold-out crowd in Portland, Maine. Elvis saw the tour as his counterattack to a tabloid tell-all book, written by his former bodyguards, that was grabbing headlines. But Elvis had ballooned to 250 pounds, and he was worried about what his fans would think of him.

On his last full day, August 15, he played with nine-year-old Lisa Marie and spent time with his twenty-year-old girlfriend, Ginger Alden, who strongly reminded those in Elvis' inner circle of Priscilla. After a brief visit to his dentist, Elvis, Ginger, and selected acquaintances stayed at the Graceland estate, discussing the tour and playing

racquetball. The night ended at 6 a.m. when Elvis and Ginger headed to bed.

Over the next two hours, Elvis consumed three packets of pills containing tranquilizers such as Placidyl and Valium and painkillers like Demerol. Agitated and unable to sleep, Elvis got out of bed around 9:00 a.m., telling Ginger that he was going to go read in the bathroom. She warned him not to fall asleep and then went back to sleep herself. At approximately 2:20 p.m., Ginger awoke to find Elvis had not come back to bed. She got up and warily entered the bathroom where Elvis' body was slumped on the floor with his face buried in the thick carpet.

Despite Elvis' bluish color and signs of rigor-mortis, his assistants administered mouth-to-mouth resuscitation and called an ambulance.

Medical technicians frantically worked on Elvis on the way to the hospital. Having heard over police scanners that an ambulance had been dispatched to Graceland, reporters arrived at Baptist Memorial Hospital ahead of Elvis. Hospital administrators kept the press at bay as doctors worked for thirty minutes to revive him. Their efforts were useless: doctors pronounced him dead of cardiac arrhythmia.

Radio stations responded immediately to the news by interrupting their regular formats to play the King's music and talk with grieving fans. Crowds in front of Graceland swelled to an estimated seventy-five thousand. Before long, movies, television specials, and books about Elvis would begin their inexorable march through popular culture, a deification process that continues to this day.

Left to right:
Thousands responded to headlines proclaiming Elvis' death by waiting in line outside Graceland for hours to view his body • Fans wait outside Graceland for a chance to pay their respects • Twenty years after his death, fans continue to decorate Elvis' grave with flowers

Crowds in front of Graceland swelled to an estimated seventy-five thousand.

Iran Hostage
Crisis

Left to right:
Iranian students parade a blindfolded American hostage through Teheran • An anti-American demonstration outside the American embassy • In one of many anti-American demonstrations held in Teheran, protesters wave a burning American flag

Iranian Shah Muhammad Reza Pahlevi, whose family had ruled Iran for decades, was overthrown in a popular revolution in 1979 and succeeded by a government headed by the Ayatollah Ruhollah Khomeini. Khomeini, a Shiite Muslim religious leader, and his followers were angry at America for supporting the Shah's regime, and when Pahlevi was allowed to enter the United States for medical reasons in October 1979, their anger exploded. On November 4, 1979, five hundred Iranian students stormed the United States embassy in the capital city of Teheran, taking more than sixty Americans hostage.

Khomeini endorsed their actions and demanded that the U.S. return the Shah to Iran as a condition to the hostages' release. President Jimmy Carter rejected that demand and struck back both militarily and financially by freezing the considerable Iranian assets in the U.S. and dispatching a naval detachment to the Indian Ocean within striking distance of Iran. It marked the beginning of a thirteen-month standoff that would outlive both Carter's presidency and even the Shah himself.

Television coverage in both countries was exhaustive. Iranian viewers watched frequent interviews with the hostages who desperately attempted to relay messages home. In the U.S., the *CBS Evening News with Walter Cronkite* ended each telecast with a tally detailing how long the hostages had been held. The ABC television network aired a late-night news program, *The Iranian Crisis: America Held Hostage*, hosted by broadcast journalist Ted Koppel. Night after night, American audiences watched the hordes of protesting Iranians burning American flags and dragging blindfolded hostages through the streets.

The challenge of America's superiority by a smaller country in the midst of revolution shocked the U.S. public. Citizens knew their only form of recourse lay with official negotiators, so they did what little they could by showing their hope and support of a peaceful solution with yellow ribbons.

Mediators worked overtime with little progress. Their one breakthrough came just before Thanksgiving Day when more than a dozen women and African American hostages were freed. After that, however, negotiations deteriorated.

The hostage situation hung like a pall over the Carter presidency. Pressure mounted for the U.S. government to somehow force a resolution to the crisis. After months of fruitless negotiations, President Carter decided to gamble on a covert military operation to free the hostages. The top-secret expedition was staged at a desert location 275 miles southeast of Teheran, and involved one hundred men. The mission took a disastrous turn when a decision was made to abort due to equipment failure, and a collision between aircraft occurred during their hurried nighttime withdrawal, killing eight American servicemen.

A defeated President Carter faced television cameras, and thus the nation, to explain the failed mission.

American audiences watched protesting Iranians burning American flags and dragging blindfolded hostages through the streets.

WELCOME BACK TO FREEDOM

He assured his viewers that the mission had not been planned as punishment to Iran, but as a last resort to free the hostages. He would not attempt another such raid. Meanwhile, Iranians celebrated the unsuccessful rescue in a rally outside the American embassy.

While negotiations continued, America was in the middle of a presidential election, and Jimmy Carter was in the fight of his political life against Republican challenger Ronald Reagan. Deputy Secretary of State Warren Christopher was racing to finish negotiations and free the hostages before Election Day. Despite strong efforts, the Carter administration fell short of its deadline. By the time the U.S. and Iran finally agreed on a satisfactory exchange, Reagan had gained the presidency in a landslide victory.

On the morning of January 20, 1981, the nation prepared for Reagan's inauguration. Meanwhile, the U.S. had agreed to return $8 billion in Iranian assets in exchange for the freedom of the American captives. A misinterpretation of the agreement's appendix by Iran's chief negotiator caused a delay in the proceedings, but the misunderstanding was quickly ironed out. Word of an imminent release was first broadcast to the nation while the Marine Band was performing

during the opening inaugural ceremonies. Shortly after Reagan's swearing in, the hostages were put on a plane and flown to West Germany. President Reagan asked Carter to fly to Germany and represent the nation in welcoming the hostages to freedom.

Their return to the U.S. after 444 days in captivity was marked across the country by expressions of joy and relief—tempered perhaps by the hard-earned knowledge that for all its military power, the United States was, like all other peoples and nations, subject to events beyond its control.

Left to right:
Demonstrators hold signs supporting the Ayatollah and blasting America • Trees outside the U.S. State Department in Washington, D.C., bear yellow ribbons to show support of a peaceful end to the hostage crisis • Hostages step off a plane and into freedom after 444 days in captivity

John Lennon
Assassinated

December 8
1980

Left to right:
The Beatles entering
a concert venue,
August 1964: (from left)
Paul McCartney, John
Lennon, Ringo Starr,
and George Harrison •
Yoko Ono and John
Lennon • The Dakota
apartment building

Like Elvis Presley, the Beatles and their music became a symbol of a period marked by profound changes in popular culture. Traveling to America three months after the tragic murder of John F. Kennedy, they became the new messengers of his optimistic vision. But unlike Elvis, the Beatles were seasoned professionals who had a mission to capture America. They knew what they wanted and they went after it with a mixture of wit, exuberance, and no small amount of musical brilliance. They did not create the 1960s cultural revolution, but they became its icon, epitomizing its searching spirit and giving popular music a depth of commitment that became linked with the social ferment of the times.

At the height of the Beatles' fame in 1965, John Lennon, the most outspoken of the four, aroused irate reactions around the world by suggesting that the band had become more popular than Jesus Christ. His observation underscored an emerging truth: the messages articulated by entertainers were often more influential, particularly with the young, than the pronouncements of traditional political and religious figures.

Despite their enormous popularity, the group began to splinter in late 1967. The Beatles held together through the summer of 1969 to record what would become their final album, *Abbey Road*. The official end came on April 10, 1970, when Paul McCartney announced he was leaving the group. With his wife, Yoko Ono, John embarked on a solo career. His post-Beatles compositions included "Imagine," "Mind Games," and "Give Peace a Chance." John and Yoko attracted considerable attention with their bed-ins, happenings, and full-page ads declaring "War Is Over!" John also fought with the U.S. government to avoid deportation. He prevailed in the courts in 1975 and settled in his adopted hometown of New York City.

For the next five years, John lived quietly as a self-described "house husband" and father, raising the couple's son, Sean Ono Lennon. By 1980 he was anxious to get back to his music, and in December, John released his first album in six years, *Double Fantasy*.

On the night of December 8, 1980, after spending five hours in the studio, John and Yoko returned home just before 11:00 p.m. to the exclusive Dakota apartment building. Waiting on the sidewalk in front of the Dakota that evening was twenty-five-year-old Mark David Chapman. Fans often waited outside the Dakota, so his presence was unremarkable. John stepped out of his limousine and was walking toward the door when a man's voice called out, "Mr. Lennon?" As John turned his head toward the voice, Chapman

A man's voice called out, "Mr. Lennon?" As John turned his head toward the voice, he was shot five times.

Top to bottom:
Mark David Chapman, shown here in his 1973 high school yearbook photo, shot Lennon at point-blank range • Fans attend a memorial in Central Park, Manhattan

approached, drew his revolver, and shot Lennon five times, striking him mostly in his arm and back. John staggered up the six steps to the entrance of the Dakota, moaning, "I'm shot, I'm shot," and then collapsed. The doorman pressed an alarm button and the police arrived within minutes. John was bleeding profusely, so rather than wait for an ambulance, the police rushed him to Roosevelt Hospital in their car. Despite doctors' efforts, John Lennon died of massive blood loss.

As news of John Lennon's murder broke, the airwaves around the world were filled with his music. Millions of Americans were watching the New England Patriots and Miami Dolphins on ABC television's *Monday Night Football*. Commentator Howard Cosell announced the tragic news. For fans of Lennon's generation, it resonated with the impact of John F. Kennedy's assassination, for it was Lennon who gave voice to their anger and frustration and clarity to their rebelliousness.

At his formal arraignment on the following day, Mark David Chapman was accused by the district attorney of coming to New York with the specific purpose of deliberately executing John Lennon. Chapman was eventually sentenced to between twenty years and life imprisonment.

Left:
People gather at
Strawberry Fields to
remember Lennon
on what would have
been his 50th birthday,
October 9, 1990.
Strawberry Fields is
an area in Central
Park near the Dakota
that pays tribute to
Lennon and his work

President Reagan *Shot*

1981

In early 1981, President Ronald Reagan and the American people were still enjoying the honeymoon from his recent election victory. But even in such times when the nation seems happy with their leadership, tremendously tight security measures are required to protect the president from the danger of would-be assassins.

On Monday, March 30, 1981, that ever-looming threat became a reality. Just over two months after taking office, President Reagan was speaking before the National Conference of the Building and Construction Trades Department of the AFL-CIO at the Washington Hilton Hotel. Outside the hotel, a troubled man named John Hinckley Jr. waited among the press and other onlookers seeking a glimpse of the President.

The twenty-five-year-old Hinckley had developed an obsession with actress Jodie Foster after seeing her in the film *Taxi Driver*. In his delusional state, Hinckley believed that by assassinating the recently inaugurated president he would win Foster's admiration.

At approximately 2:25 p.m., the President and his Secret Service agents exited the hotel. Approaching his awaiting motorcade, Reagan waved to well-wishers and photographers. But the scene changed quickly when Hinckley stepped out of the crowd and emptied his .22-caliber pistol in the direction of the President. The sound of gunfire crackled through the crowd, and the spray of bullets hit a District of Columbia

The bullet had stopped just one inch from his heart.

Brady was in critical condition "fighting for his life." ABC, NBC, and CBS all aired continuous coverage well into the evening.

Reagan underwent successful surgery to remove the bullet as the day progressed. From the hospital, doctors assured the media, and a worried nation, that the President "was at no time in any serious danger." He recovered quickly over the next several days, while stories of his courage and good humor in the midst of a terrifying situation became legend, further endearing him to a still shaken public.

Press Secretary James Brady's wound proved far more serious. Struck in the head, the gunshot left him paralyzed and brain damaged. Though he was unable to resume his duties as presidential press secretary, over the next twelve years Brady and his wife did return to Washington to successfully lobby for a bill imposing a five-day waiting period and criminal background check before an individual can purchase a handgun.

In a closely watched court case with repercussions for the future of the United States legal system, the twisted plot of attempted assassin John Hinckley would form the basis of his defense. A jury found him not guilty by reason of insanity. He was remanded to a high-security psychiatric hospital for an indeterminate term. As a result, the insanity plea became a more frequently used, and heavily debated, court defense for violent acts.

Clockwise from left: President Reagan waves to a crowd standing outside Washington, D.C.'s Hilton Hotel moments before the shooting • Police officer Thomas Delahanty, shot in the neck, is sprawled on the ground as James Brady, shot in the head, is attended to behind him • First Lady Nancy Reagan greets her recovering husband in the hospital • Federal marshals escort Hinckley at the Quantico Marine Base

police officer, a Secret Service agent, and Press Secretary James Brady.

On instinct, a Secret Service agent roughly pushed Reagan into his limousine, but on the way in, a bullet ricocheted off the car and struck the President. Within seconds, other police officers and Secret Service agents located the source of the gunfire and wrestled Hinckley to the ground.

Though agents did not know the President had been shot, they feared he may have suffered a broken rib when he was pushed into the car. The limo sped to George Washington University Hospital where only after his shirt had been cut away was it discovered that he had been shot. The bullet had stopped just one inch from his heart.

News of the attempted assassination broke immediately. The networks interrupted their regular programming with bulletins inaccurately reporting that the President had escaped harm but that Press Secretary James Brady was dead. It wasn't until approximately 3:43 p.m., over an hour after the attempt, that Deputy Press Secretary Lyn Nofziger briefed the press from the hospital and confirmed that Reagan had been shot and was about to undergo surgery, and James

The Challenger *Explodes*

Above:
Crew members of
the space shuttle
Challenger (clockwise from
top left): Ellison Onizuka,
Christa McAuliffe,
Gregory Jarvis, Judith
Resnick, Ronald McNair,
Francis Dick Scobee,
and Michael J. Smith

January 28
1986

It was unusually cold for south Florida on the otherwise crystal clear morning of January 28, 1986. It seemed a perfect day for a shuttle launch. For NASA, this twenty-fifth shuttle mission was to be a historical flight. This time, the *Challenger* was carrying their very first civilian passenger. A schoolteacher from Concord, New Hampshire, was going along as a representative "ordinary citizen." But the flight of the *Challenger* that day would make a tragic, rather than triumphant, entry into history.

Named for an 1870s naval research vessel, space shuttle *Challenger* joined NASA's growing fleet of reusable spaceships in July 1982. After nine successful missions, the most recent concluding on November 6, 1985, NASA had just ten weeks to prepare *Challenger* for its next flight.

In early 1986, NASA and the shuttle program were on a roll. With fifteen launches planned for the year, six more than the year

before, missions were verging on routine. In a campaign designed to revive the public's interest in the space program, NASA selected a thirty-seven-year-old high school teacher named Christa McAuliffe to journey into space with the team of six scientists and astronauts. NASA's public relations plan seemed to have the desired effect. McAuliffe was a frequent guest on radio and television talk shows, and newspapers and television news programs chronicled her every move during her astronaut training.

After four previous postponements due twice to rescheduling of the preceding mission, and once each to bad weather and a faulty hatch, NASA did not feel the frigid temperatures on the morning of the launch were reason enough to halt the final countdown.

Although shuttle launches were becoming commonplace and television audience levels were steadily declining, as anticipated, McAuliffe on

*The Challenger
was carrying the first
civilian passenger,
a teacher.*

board caused millions to tune in. Shortly after 9:00 a.m., the seven astronauts took the crew elevator twelve stories to the top of launch pad 39-B, strapped themselves into their seats, and awaited the last of the countdown.

At 11:39 a.m., *Challenger's* engines roared to life and the spacecraft lifted skyward. By television, the country simultaneously watched the liftoff, McAuliffe's cheering students, and her parents' awestruck gaze. For a few brief seconds the liftoff of the space shuttle *Challenger* was all that NASA had hoped for.

But at fifty-nine seconds after liftoff, a nearly undetectable plume of black smoke appeared from the lower right booster rocket. Unbeknownst to the ground or flight crews, a crucial O-ring that sealed the booster rockets had split.

Challenger was now traveling at a speed of twenty-nine hundred feet per second. The flight

Left to right:
The *Challenger* crew smiles at waiting crowds as they walk to the launch pad • The doomed space shuttle fires up for liftoff

"The Challenger crew was pulling us into the future and we'll continue to follow them."

Left to right:
At seventy-four seconds into its flight, the *Challenger* exploded over the Atlantic Ocean • Christa McAuliffe's parents and sister react to the explosion

looked good, and mission control gave Commander Francis Scobee permission to increase to full power. "Roger, go with throttle up," answered Scobee. At seventy-four seconds into the flight, catastrophe struck. The black smoke from the fractured O-rings became a burst of flames, setting off a quick succession of explosions, climaxing with the *Challenger* erupting into an enormous fireball and disintegrating over the Atlantic Ocean.

The cheering in the Concord classroom turned to stunned silence, and the look of pride and wonderment on the faces of McAuliffe's parents quickly changed to confusion, and then to horror. Air and sea rescue teams were dispatched, but there would be no recovery.

That night, President Ronald Reagan canceled the scheduled State of the Union address, and instead spoke to the nation about the tragedy from the Oval Office. In an attempt to console a grieving nation, the President said, "I know it's hard to understand, but sometimes painful things like this happen. It's all part of the process of exploration and discovery. The future doesn't belong to the fainthearted; it belongs to the brave. The *Challenger* crew was pulling us into the future and we'll continue to follow them."

In their 256-page report, former Secretary of State William Rogers and a thirteen-member presidential commission assigned to determine the cause of the disaster laid the blame on defective O-ring seals, which NASA admitted had been a concern but did nothing about. NASA's director was summarily fired, and the shuttle program was put on hold indefinitely. The vision of the *Challenger* exploding in full view on television seemed to sap the national will toward future missions. It would be thirty-two months before there would be another shuttle launch.

Berlin Wall *Crumbles*

1989

Since 1945, the power of nuclear weapons changed the rules of war. The stakes of war had simply become too high. Conventional battles gave way to "cold" war and political ideologies became the new weapons of mass destruction, with freedom and dignity its casualties.

As they had after World War I, Allied leaders met at the end of the Second World War to determine Germany's fate. This time, they were resolute to ensure Germany would not be left with the capabilities to begin another global conflict. As a result, this European Advisory Commission—representing the United States, Soviet Union, Britain, and France—divided Germany into four zones. The division, supposedly temporary, allowed for the occupation of Germany by each of the Allied countries for the purpose of rebuilding the destroyed landscape and economy. Although it was completely surrounded by the Soviet-occupied zone, the former capital, Berlin,

was left to joint control—it too was divided into four sectors.

But while zones occupied by Western powers enjoyed rebuilding efforts, democratic self-government, and capitalist economies, the Soviet zone was being punished. Soviet troops dismantled the industries and remaining riches in the East sector, taking the spoils back to the U.S.S.R. as payment for damages suffered during the war. A Soviet-sanctioned government dictated the lives of its citizens and planted the seeds of communism.

By 1948, the Western powers had united their zones, hoping to create a new and independent West Germany that included Berlin. A West German currency was issued and plans were made to introduce the new German mark into Berlin. The Soviets opposed West Germany's currency in Berlin, however, and began a move to force the Allies out of the city. What began as restricted

Soldiers with shoot-to-kill orders swarmed the border as frantic citizens attempted to escape.

access from West Germany to West Berlin ended in a crippling blockade. On June 24, 1948, Soviets cut transportation, communication, food, and living supplies to the city, expecting the Western powers to give up and leave. Exactly the opposite occurred: the West answered the blockade with massive airlifts. Planes loaded with supplies and fuel landed in Berlin approximately every three minutes. The airlift continued until the blockade was lifted the following May.

The Soviets' concession regarding the blockade was in no way close to surrender. Tensions mounted over the next decade so that by November 1958 Soviet Premier Nikita Khrushchev offered an ultimatum with a six-month time limit. Western powers could evacuate Berlin, leaving it to East Germany but under the control of the United Nations, or East Germany would strongarm its control over the Western sectors and force out occupying troops. The Western powers rejected this "free city" plan, calling Khrushchev's

bluff. Three years later, a June 1961 meeting between Khrushchev and American President John F. Kennedy did little but widen the gap between East and West, communism and capitalism.

Meanwhile, East German citizens continued to pour into West Germany and West Berlin. Those leaving their homes did so in hope of better, more prosperous lives. In East Berlin alone, from January 1961 to the beginning of the following August, an estimated two hundred thousand people left for the opportunities and intellectual freedom offered in the West.

Such an exodus worried East Berlin's leader, Walter Ulbricht, who believed a wall between East and West Berlin would both prevent his citizens from leaving for the West and send a strong message to his capitalist neighbor.

Zero hour occurred shortly after midnight on August 13, 1961. The border that had once been set by World War II's Allied leaders for the welfare of Berlin, now stood as concrete and barbed wire,

Left to right:
Construction of the Berlin Wall began shortly after midnight on August 13, 1961 • The Checkpoint Charlie facility was the main crossing point for American officials • East and West Berlin guards face off through the barbed wire that separates their city • A bus carrying several East Germans attempts to break through the Sandkrug Bridge crossing, May 1963

East Berlin border guards stand at the Brandenburg Gate while West Berliners mill in front of the graffiti-riddled wall • A West Berlin man chisels his way through the wall after the East German government announced it would open its borders • A German citizen flashes the "peace" sign as people pour through an opening in the wall • Berliners celebrate atop the wall at the Brandenburg Gate

separating a community. East German guards and Soviet troops cut telephone wires and halted transportation between the city's two sides. Soldiers with shoot-to-kill orders swarmed the border as frantic citizens attempted last-minute escapes.

In its completed stage, the Berlin Wall stretched twenty-eight miles through the center of the city. A shadow wall separated East Berliners from the main wall structure, forcing potential escapees to break through two walls while avoiding attack dogs, armed gunmen, and minefields. Thirty thousand heavily armed troops stood guard from nearly four hundred positions.

East Germany worked double-time to control its citizens, but it had absolutely no leverage when it came to activities on the other side of the

wall. The non-communist West used West Berlin as a soapbox to exalt freedom's attributes. President Kennedy traveled to Berlin in June 1963, standing in the shadow of the wall to speak to an enthusiastic crowd of one hundred fifty thousand people. He reassured them that Berlin was not alone in its struggle: "All free men, wherever they may live, are citizens of Berlin. And therefore, as a free man, I take pride in the words, 'Ich bin ein Berliner.' (I am a Berliner.)"

Though the wall still divided East and West twenty-four years after Kennedy's declaration, the two superpowers worked toward a peaceful resolution to the cold war. Though the biting rhetoric of the previous forty years was not always absent from negotiation, President Ronald Reagan and

Scores of young East and West Germans climbed to the top of the wall to greet each other and celebrate.

Left to right:
Friends and relatives reunite after twenty-eight years of forced separation • Lasers and fireworks entertain a crowd of millions who gather at the Brandenburg Gate to celebrate German reunification, October 3, 1990

General Secretary Mikhail Gorbachev expressed an eagerness to make amends. But before U.S. and Soviet ideologies could mix, the physical barriers had to be broken. From the wall, Reagan voiced the potential of positive U.S.–Soviet relations and the value of liberty. He challenged Gorbachev to "tear down this wall."

Whether or not a direct answer to Reagan's plea, Gorbachev initiated the policies that set cracks in the Berlin Wall. His policies of *glasnost*, which released emigration controls and supported human rights, and *perestroika*, which increased the citizens' role in government, helped Soviet bloc countries that were flailing in crumbled economies. As a result, Soviet-controlled countries began to once again open their borders.

On the evening of November 9, 1989, the East German government announced in a press conference that the border between East and West Berlin would be opened. East Germany hoped that by offering unconditional passage to West Berlin, its people would take advantage of travel opportunities but would ultimately return to the East.

Bulletins flashed on radio and television around the world. Networks aired coverage of this historic event and showed pictures of the hundreds of jubilant East Berliners pouring into West Berlin for their first visits to the western half of the city in twenty-eight years. Scores of young East and West Germans climbed to the top of the wall to greet each other and celebrate, using small hammers and chisels to chip away at the wall. Fireworks exploded over West Berlin's main boulevard in an impromptu street festival that lasted into the early hours of the morning.

The opening of Berlin's borders and the subsequent destruction of the wall also opened plans for German reunification. On October 3, 1990, Germany officially became whole again.

Fireworks exploded over West Berlin's main boulevard in an impromptu street festival.

Operation Desert Storm *Begins*

January 29
1991

Top to bottom:
Saddam Hussein waves to supporters • General Norman Schwarzkof met with the ever-present media continually

After 1989, the Soviet Union began to crack apart into independent republics; the cold war was over and its accompanying fears and nuclear threats dissipated. But in 1991, a new conflict with global implications arose in the Middle East.

Iraqi President Saddam Hussein, long considered an adversary by most of the Arab world, accused the neighboring countries of Kuwait and the United Arab Emirates of conspiring with America and Israel to exceed oil production in order to drive down the price of oil. Iraq had accumulated an $80 billion debt as a result of its war with Iran, and hoped to offset it by inflating oil prices, but other gulf leaders refused to support his

scheme. On July 17, 1990, Hussein publicly threatened war, but his behavior was shrugged off as mere posturing to gain leverage over Kuwait in the oil-pricing debate.

On August 2, Saddam Hussein gave credence to his word and ordered his forces into Kuwait. In less than one week, he declared it an annex of the Iraqi nation, and began positioning tanks and artillery along the northern borders of Saudi Arabia.

On Wednesday, August 8, President George Bush took his concerns to the American people in a nationally televised address, castigating Hussein's invasion of Kuwait as a deliberate act of "naked aggression,"

Just as the military was preparing for an all-out war, so was the media.

Bernard Shaw
CNN Reporting

Baghdad, Iraq

and a direct threat to the economic interests of the United States. Bush announced that he was sending troops and drawing "a line in the sand" against Iraqi aggression. To back up his admonition, the President launched Operation Desert Shield, the largest multinational military operation since the Allied D-Day invasion of Europe.

Months of military strategizing and diplomatic maneuvering culminated on November 29,

when the United Nations Security Council sanctioned the use of force if Iraq did not leave Kuwait by January 15. The fuse of war was lit. The incendiary rhetoric between Hussein and Bush continued as tensions in the region boiled, and Iraqi forces showed no sign of withdrawing.

The military buildup for Desert Shield continued at a staggering rate. In only six months the U.S. presence in the gulf nearly matched that of Vietnam

Left to right:
Overnight bombing leaves Baghdad in flames. U.S officials said they targeted military sites, with little damage to civilian areas • CNN correspondent Bernard Shaw reports back to America the events of the war

at the height of the war. Every dock and airfield in the Saudi kingdom was overflowing with American equipment, ammunition, and supplies.

Just as the military was preparing for an all-out war, so was the media. The major television and radio networks began strategically placing crews throughout the Desert Shield theater. However, CNN was the only news source that had secured a dedicated 4-wire phone line into their Baghdad bureau.

Hussein ignored the deadline to abandon his occupation of Kuwait. On the evening of January 16, 1991, regular radio and television programming was abruptly pre-empted, and President Bush told the nation that war had begun. Operation Desert Shield became Operation Desert Storm.

Employing devastating air power, the United States hit Iraq with tens of thousands of bombs.

Flying virtually undetected, sophisticated U.S. Air Force F-117 Stealth fighter jets dropped laser-guided "smart bombs" on the Iraqi capital of Baghdad. Although their dedicated 4-wire line only permitted voice transmission, CNN correspondents John Holliman, Bernard Shaw, and Peter Arnett scooped their competition by broadcasting the initial bombardment live. Images of the aerial nighttime raid, which seemed lit with the strange phosphorescence of a video game, were transmitted out the next day. For the first time in its history, America listened to a war at the moment it began.

In retaliation for the attack, Iraq launched its Scud missiles not only against U.S. encampments in Saudi Arabia, but also against cities in Israel. Networks broadcast the attacks live from Israel, most notably with NBC correspondent Arthur Kent

Left to right:
A U.S. marine searches an abandoned Kuwaiti town • An Israeli man and his son sit in the debris that was once their home after it was hit by an Iraqi Scud missile • Iraqi soldiers loiter in front of a war-damaged mosque in the holy city of Karbala

Once again, television had demonstrated its ability to mold public opinion by either exposing or inoculating viewers to the true horrors of war.

Left to right:
Oil fires lit the Iraqi horizon for months after the war had ended • Iraqi soldiers surrender to U.S. forces along a highway • Thousands of vehicles on the highway between Kuwait City and Iraq were destroyed in bombings. An American soldier looks at the wreckage

reporting from atop buildings as missiles flashed overhead.

Within the first forty-eight hours, Desert Storm bombers had completed a merciless 850 missions, blasting Hussein's power plants, airfields, radar installations, and missile sites. Even the Iraqi President's heavily fortified lakeside palace in Baghdad was destroyed.

The air attacks severely weakened Iraqi troops, setting them up for a ground attack which would push them from Kuwait in just one

hundred hours. Operation Desert Storm resulted in the most one-sided victory in modern military history. A total of 148 U.S. soldiers were killed in action. The coalition command estimated that two hundred thousand Iraqis were killed. But if the effects seemed bloodless and unreal to viewers watching from America, they wreaked genuine havoc on Iraqi soldiers and citizens. Once again, television had demonstrated its ability to mold public opinion by either exposing or inoculating viewers to the true horrors of war.

Rodney King Verdict
Incites Riots

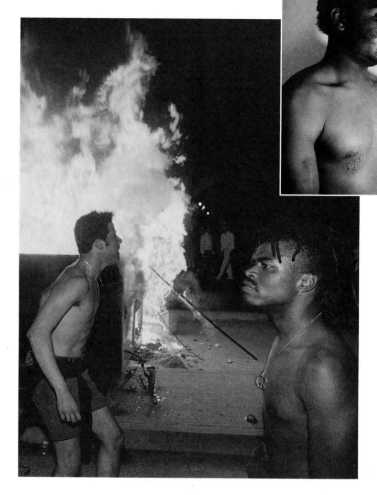

April 29
1992

On March 3, 1991, what should have been a routine traffic stop of a motorist led to terrifying riots and the utter destruction of much of greater Los Angeles.

An eighty-one-second videotape of the incident showed African American motorist Rodney G. King being beaten by white Los Angeles Police Department Officers Laurence Powell, Theodore J. Briseno, Timothy E. Wind, and Sgt. Stacey C. Koon. King had led the officers on a high-speed chase through L.A. and then allegedly resisted arrest. The encounter ended with King lying semiconscious on the ground as the four officers continued to kick and club him. Broadcast repeatedly over the next fourteen months, the tape divided viewers into two camps: those who thought King unnecessarily refused to follow the police instructions and was therefore subject to reasonable restraint, and those who thought King was mercilessly, brutally beaten.

Although the event took place in the City and County of Los Angeles, the trial of the accused police officers took place in Simi Valley in Ventura County, north of L.A. There was considerable protest over the decision to move the trial to the predominantly white community that was home to many police professionals, and fears were realized when the jury selected included ten white citizens, one Latina, and one Asian American.

The three-month trial included testimony from fifty-five witnesses. The infamous videotape was shown to the jury numerous times.

The Ventura County Superior Court jury deliberated for seven days. The first few days of deliberation focused on a single count of assault on Officer Powell, but the jury could not reach a consensus, and Judge Stanley M. Weisberg declared a mistrial on that count. The remaining days of deliberation were spent reviewing all other counts.

"The city's erupted over the 'not guilty' verdict."

On Wednesday, April 29, 1992, the courthouse was at full capacity and silent with anticipation as the verdict was announced: all four defendants were acquitted.

All races felt betrayed by the verdict. Many said the jurors could not have seen and heard the same evidence shown to the rest of the world. But no answers were forthcoming about the jurors' reasoning: the members of the six-man, six-woman jury, sequestered during deliberations, refused to speak to the press after the verdict was announced.

The verdict bulletins that interrupted regular television and radio broadcasting segued into all-day, all-night coverage of a city's citizens enraged by the verdict.

The nation watched the destruction of Los Angeles on live television. News helicopters hovered over the streets, recording senseless beatings, looting, and arson. Violence erupted at the corners of Florence and Normandie in South Central L.A. where people were pulled from their cars and attacked. The rioting and destruction soon spread to other, distant areas of the city, with more than 150 fires raging across greater Los Angeles. Smoke in the South L.A. area became so thick that the Federal Aviation Authority ordered the rerouting of flights into Los Angeles International Airport.

Left to right:
Rioters outside the Los Angeles Police Department headquarters protest the trial's outcome • Rodney King was severly beaten by four police officers. His body shows the scars three days after the incident • Arson fires obliterate a Los Angeles city block • Citizens loot a strip mall in Los Angeles, April 30, 1992

Above:
Helicopter pilot Bob Tur hovered over rioters who pulled truck driver Reginald Denny out of his vehicle, beat him, and left him unconscious in the street. Denny survived the incident and his assailants later were caught due to the helicopter camera footage

In downtown Los Angeles, protesters stormed police headquarters, as well as City Hall, the *Los Angeles Times* building, courthouses, and government office buildings. Mobs threw broken bottles and pieces of concrete at bystanders and passing motorists, leaving blazing fires in their wake.

Shortly after 11 p.m., Mayor Bradley appeared on television to say that the city would "take whatever resources needed" to squelch the violence. He reported that the Los Angeles Police Department was being assisted by the L.A. County Sheriff's Department, the California Highway Patrol, and police and fire departments from neighboring cities. Governor Pete Wilson ordered the National Guard to report for duty. On Thursday afternoon, National Guardsmen armed with M-16 rifles had taken positions in locations of the deadliest violence.

The city had reached a peak of racial division, with merchants, protesters, and looters of all races pitted against each other.

By the early evening of Thursday, April 30, looting had spread, with marauders carrying off everything from diapers to big screen televisions. Parents brought their children to help carry the stolen goods, and a number of grocery stores were decimated. A curfew of 8:00 p.m. was enforced city-wide.

Fearing the effects of violence, the U. S. Post Office suspended mail delivery to fourteen zip codes, all city schools were closed, and trash collection was delayed.

Professional sports teams canceled their games, including an NBA playoff between the L.A. Clippers and the Utah Jazz. Final exams at USC were postponed, and classes at UCLA were canceled.

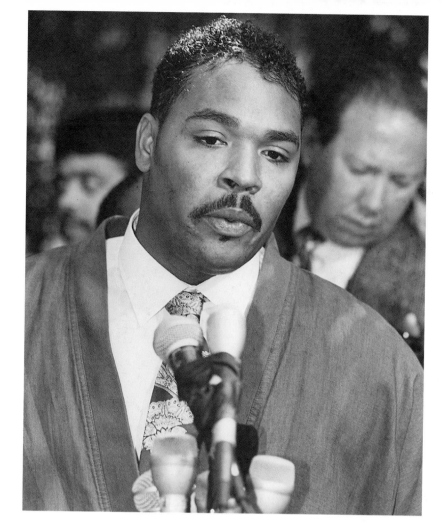

"Can't we all get along?"

Other cities across the nation, large and small, also reeled from the effects of the verdict, reporting random looting and smashed storefronts. Demonstrators closed the Oakland Bay-San Francisco Bridge, one person was killed in Las Vegas, and in Atlanta, Martin Luther King Jr.'s hometown, a peaceful protest turned to violence. Comedian Bill Cosby made a televised plea for everyone to go home and watch *The Cosby Show* that night instead of running wild in the streets.

By the weekend, Los Angeles and its residents were recovering from the terror of the preceding nights. The riots had caused at least fifty deaths, including eight people shot by police. Over two thousand injuries were reported, more than one hundred of them critical. The National Guard supplied six thousand troops, with another 750 coming from the California Highway Patrol.

In all, authorities recorded more than seven hundred arrests. Nearly eighteen hundred firefighters were deployed to extinguish more than one thousand fires. City-wide damage estimates neared $1 billion.

In the months that followed, Los Angeles attempted to rebuild its scorched infrastructure and its bruised racial relations. A later federal trial of Sgt. Koon and Officer Powell would result in the guilty verdict many felt was cheated from them in the first trial.

But the riots had already left their scars, and they left the world with two images indelibly etched in the public consciousness: live coverage of what seemed to be all of Los Angeles burning in the night, and the plaintive appeal of Rodney King himself pleading, "Can't we all get along?"

Above:
Rodney King addresses the press, and greater Los Angeles, at a conference following two days of rioting

Waco Standoff
Ends in Disaster

April 19
1993

Left to right:
Charismatic cult leader
David Koresh •
The Branch Davidian
compound outside
Waco, Texas • ATF
agents gather at the FBI
command center

Though the Branch Davidian community had existed in various forms outside the Texas town of Waco for nearly sixty years, the group's final leader, David Koresh, brought the cult to infamy. Beginning as an offshoot of the Seventh Day Adventist Church, the Branch Davidians refined and redefined themselves over the decades, strongly maintaining an apocalyptic theology throughout. Koresh seized leadership of the sect in the late 1980s, preaching that the end of the world would occur after a deadly battle with non-believers. For eighty-six members of the Branch Davidians, he was right.

Koresh led his followers with a golden tongue and an iron fist—both in preparation for the ultimate battle for religious salvation. His lectures and prophecies were relayed via hours upon hours of lecture and audio-taped Bible study. His impassioned speeches spoke to members of the need to ready themselves for the apocalypse. To

his followers, Koresh's word was the word of God. And Koresh himself agreed, saying to them, "If the Bible is true, then I'm Christ."

At its strongest, the cult had a membership of 130 men, women, and children, each preparing for battle. All members followed strict diets and military-style conditioning. Men trained in combat while women practiced more domestic chores. Koresh taught his followers that it was his right, and his alone, to procreate, giving the title of "wife" to several women in the cult—some as young as twelve years old.

By 1992, the arsenal of weapons and ammunition Koresh had amassed for his version of Armageddon had attracted the attention of the Bureau of Alcohol, Tobacco, and Firearms (ATF). Anticipating there was illegal possession of firearms and explosives by Davidian members, one hundred agents raided the compound with search and arrest warrants on February 28, 1993.

"If the Bible is true, then I'm Christ."

But cult members were waiting for the agents' arrival and the ensuing gun battle left four federal agents and as many as six Davidians dead.

The siege marked the beginning of a fifty-one-day standoff where ATF agents desperately attempted to drive Koresh and his followers from the compound. Electricity and telephone lines were cut, floodlights glared in the windows day and night, and loudspeakers broadcast deafening, irritating music and sounds of rabbits being slaughtered. Thirty-seven people, twenty-one of them children, emerged from the fortress and turned themselves over to federal agents.

Koresh negotiated with the ATF as a prophet, insisting that resolution to the conflict would come on his own terms. In letters to agents he stated his position, "I AM your God and you will bow under my feet....Do you think you have power to stop My will?... My hand made heaven and earth, My hand also shall bring it to the end."

Still, he vowed a peaceful surrender several times, only to break his promises once his conditions were granted. His last condition, that he could finish a lengthy manuscript on the Seven Seals of the Book of Revelation before surrender, was never met. The agents had run out of patience and were meeting with Attorney General Janet Reno for permission to use force and end the standoff.

Reno, with only a month on the job, was resolute to ensure all peaceful possibilities had been exhausted. She worried about the effect a raid would have on the seventeen children in the compound. But reports that the children were being beaten and fear that certain members would use them as human shields in a gun battle forced her hand—waiting any longer could cost lives. Reno consented to a plan for tanks to puncture holes in the compound's buildings, allowing both a place for agents to throw in non-lethal tear gas and an area for members to exit and surrender.

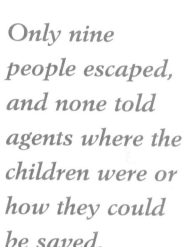

Only nine people escaped, and none told agents where the children were or how they could be saved.

Agents waited for the wind to subside on the morning of April 19, 1993, so the tear gas plan would be at full effect. Finally, shortly after 6 a.m., armored vehicles began ramming the Branch Davidian compound. "This is not an assault," roared the speakers aimed at the fort. "Do not shoot. We are not entering your compound." Meanwhile, agents warned those inside via telephone of their plan, wanting to make sure children would not be hit by debris from damaged walls or falling tear gas canisters. The cult members answered by donning gas masks, firing at the vehicles, and then going about their daily chores.

Six hours and eighteen bottles of tear gas later, little had been accomplished. But just after noon, smoke began pouring from the buildings. Though ambulances had been dispatched to the area, there were no firetrucks nearby and all the agents could do was watch as the wood-constructed compound went up in flames. Only nine people stumbled from the buildings, and none told agents where the children were or how they could be saved.

Reno took full responsibility for the siege and its tragic finale. She publicly admitted via television and radio that, in retrospect, the plan was flawed. Regardless of how the fires began—a topic that still draws controversy—agents should have been prepared for such a disaster. More important, perhaps there existed another more peaceful way to end the stalemate.

Of the nine survivors, eight were convicted on charges stemming from the failed February 28 raid. Those convicted received sentences ranging from five to forty years. The ninth survivor received a three-year prison term in exchange for her testimony.

Left to right:
Fires broke out from within the compound after ATF agents bombarded the buildings with tear gas. Eighty-six men, women, and children perished • FBI agents inspect a cinder-block bunker left standing after the siege • A water tank, bunker, and swimming pool are all that is left of the Branch Davidians' compound

O.J. Simpson
Saga

June 13
1994
– Through –
February 4
1997

Above:
O.J. Simpson with wife
Nicole and family

Orenthal James "O.J." Simpson first came to national attention as a running back at the University of Southern California, winning college football's highest honor, the Heisman Trophy. Going on to play professionally with the Buffalo Bills, O.J. became the first National Football League running back to gain more than two thousand yards in one season and was later elected to the football Hall of Fame.

Simpson also ran his way to a lucrative endorsement with Hertz Rent-A-Car, showed off his comedy talents in the movie *The Naked Gun*, and appeared as a television analyst for the NFL. He had money, fame, a beautiful wife Nicole, and children he loved. O.J. Simpson had everything, but it would all change on June 13, 1994.

It was past midnight when police were called to the West Los Angeles condominium of Nicole Brown Simpson. In the front courtyard, they found her body and the body of Ronald Goldman.

The previous evening, Nicole's mother noticed her glasses were missing and assumed she'd left them at Mezzaluna, the West Los Angeles restaurant where the family had dined. Waiter and acquaintance Ron Goldman found the glasses and volunteered to drop them off at Nicole's home that evening. It would later appear that an unknown assailant brutally murdered the two just after Ron arrived at Nicole's home.

Just before midnight pacific standard time, O.J. Simpson flew to Chicago, where he was contacted early Monday morning by local police. He immediately flew back to Los Angeles, and, on Thursday, attended Nicole's funeral, with his young children Sydney and Justin at his side. Suspicion mounted that O.J. Simpson was the killer, but he remained free, fanning the flames of controversy that a non-celebrity suspect would already have been in custody. During a Friday, June 17 press conference, Los Angeles Police

Television viewers watched the broadcast of the bizarre, slow-speed chase across Los Angeles freeways.

Department Commander David Gascon denied that O.J. had received special treatment, saying that there had been no "rush to judgment," a phrase that would appear repeatedly throughout the next eighteen months.

Gascon's press conference took place on the day that O.J. Simpson had agreed to surrender to police custody. At 8:30 a.m., police had reached defense attorney Robert Shapiro at his home, notifying him that they officially considered Simpson a murder suspect. Shapiro agreed to produce Simpson at police headquarters at 11 a.m. When, at nearly noon, O.J. still hadn't appeared, the LAPD declared him a fugitive and Gascon anounced a "statewide manhunt,"

Clockwise from left:
Charged with the double murder of his wife and an acquaintance, Simpson led police on a ninety-minute car chase through Los Angeles freeways. The slow-speed chase attracted the attention of local bystanders and of national television viewers • Simpson friend and former teammate Al Cowlings drove Simpson around Los Angeles until the accused eventually surrendered • Los Angeles Police Department booking photo of Simpson following his arrest for two murders, June 17, 1994

Left to right:
Simpson models the
bloody gloves that were
used in the murders. He
claimed the gloves were
too tight • With his
lawyer, Johnnie Cochran,
Simpson celebrates
his acquittal

eliciting an audible gasp from the assembled members of the press. This latest news hit the airwaves like a bomb, stunning the nation.

A few hours later, O.J. Simpson was spotted traveling in the rear of his white Ford Bronco with his lifelong friend and former teammate Al Cowlings in the driver's seat. Across the nation, viewers watched dumbfounded as the coverage of a nationally televised basketball playoff game was interrupted by the broadcast of the bizarre, slow-speed chase across Los Angeles freeways. Police cars and helicopters followed O.J. and Cowlings, who pleaded, via cellular phone, for the authorities to back off. Carrying his passport, thousands of dollars in cash, and a disguise, O.J. sat with a gun to his head. Cowlings' recorded cell phone conversations with the police revealed that Simpson was apparently on the verge of taking his own life.

The amazing live coverage of what turned into a freeway parade caused hundreds of people to line up on freeway overpasses, crying, shouting, some even holding makeshift banners showing their support of the ex-football star. Just after dark, the Bronco turned into the driveway of O.J.'s Brentwood mansion. Simpson was quietly taken into custody by the police and escorted to the county jail. O.J. Simpson, star football player,

American hero, television and movie actor, was now prisoner number BK40139700617-94.

Opening statements in Simpson's murder trial began on January 24, 1995. The ensuing trial and public reaction to it was unprecedented. As detail after detail unfolded, the twists and turns of the incredible events took over the American airwaves, with television, cable, and radio broadcasting live from inside the courtroom, then rerunning the coverage throughout the evening and on weekends.

Newspapers and magazines ran verbatim reports of testimony, courtroom gossip, and editorials about every aspect of the case. The trial was not only the top news of the day, it was almost the only news of the day.

In the early days of October 1995, prosecution and defense attorneys completed their summations. Judge Lance Ito gave his final instructions to the jurors as even the most jaded and bored trial-watchers returned to their televisions and radios, to wait for the verdict, although almost everyone seemed to think that it would be a long way off.

After only four hours of deliberation, the jury sent a shocking message to Judge Ito: they had reached a verdict. It was late in the day, and Ito decided that the verdict would be held until

A little more than a year after being acquitted in the criminal trial, the civil trial against O.J. Simpson began in the Los Angeles beachside city of Santa Monica.

The new trial was less spectacular, with little new in the way of evidence or arguments. Because the judge presiding over the civil trial prohibited cameras in the courtroom, these proceedings never commanded the intense interest or press coverage engendered by the criminal case. However, Simpson supporters were still vocal about his innocence, and those who believed him guilty hoped they would finally see justice.

On February 4, 1997, the jury was prepared to render a verdict. The press, having sat poised throughout the six-month trial, now faced a dilemma—cover the verdict and any subsequent reaction to it, or broadcast President Clinton's State of the Union address. The three major networks opted for the latter, running the verdict at the bottom of television screens just as the President was concluding his speech. Some cable television networks, however, kept their cameras outside Simpson's courthouse. Because of the media blackout inside, all court proceedings were relayed to those outside in a Morse code-like fashion of flashing cards. Though visual, the code came through loud and clear: the jury unanimously declared Simpson liable for the wrongful death of Ronald Goldman and the beatings of Nicole Brown Simpson. Both compensatory and punitive damages were awarded to the tune of $33 million.

the next morning, forcing the jury to spend one more night in sequestration and forcing the public to keep waiting for the other shoe to drop in the cliffhanger trial of the century.

The next morning, normal broadcasting was suspended as television and radio stations around the world prepared to air the verdict live. Finally, on October 3, 1995, a nervous female court clerk, stumbling on the name Orenthal James Simpson, announced to the world that the jury had found O.J. Simpson not guilty on all counts.

Not unexpectedly, the Brown and Goldman families were outraged and frustrated. The Goldman family initiated a civil suit against Simpson for the wrongful death of Ron Goldman. Nicole's parents—hoping to keep their grandchildren from testifying in a wrongful death trial—sued concerning their daughter's battery at the hands of her former husband.

Above:
Simpson supporters outside the Los Angeles courtroom react to the televised verdict in the criminal trial

Oklahoma City
Bombing

April 19
1995

Left to right:
A homemade bomb
aimed at the federal
building's second-floor
daycare center crumbled
nine stories and killed
167 people • Aerial view
of the Alfred P. Murrah
building eight days after
the bombing • Medical
assistants from a nearby
hospital rush to the scene

Oklahoma City lies in the heartland of the United States, a cosmopolitan city big enough to boast museums and a thriving downtown, yet far enough away from places like New York or Los Angeles to still embody old-fashioned American values.

The morning of Wednesday, April 19, 1995, was like any other midweek day at the Alfred P. Murrah Federal Building in Oklahoma City. Children were dropped off at the second-floor daycare center as more than 350 federal employees and visitors began work, and a busy bank of elevators rose and fell to each of the building's nine levels.

Outside, a Ryder rental truck sat near the curb just beyond the building's daycare center. The truck driver had made his getaway, leaving behind a two-ton homemade bomb made of fertilizer and fuel oil.

At 9:03 a.m., the bomb exploded and the nation's innocence shattered. A fireball shot from the truck and hit the side of the building. The explosion could be seen for thirty miles across the flat Oklahoma horizon. Half of the federal building disappeared in an instant as its debris rained down upon the neighboring blocks.

Rescue workers rushed to the site from every corner of the city. Doctors and nurses from nearby hospitals literally ran to the federal building to set up makeshift triage areas in the street. Galvanized into heroic action, men and women dug with their bare hands to try to free the hundreds buried in the bloody rubble, hoping to find anyone still alive. Throughout the day, victims wandered like zombies out into the street, some collapsing to the ground, many covered in blood and smoke. As rain began to fall, heavy machinery was brought in to lift the heaviest debris in hopes that more survivors would be found before dark.

News crews arrived on the scene almost instantaneously, broadcasting the carnage and

Half of the building disappeared in an instant as debris rained down upon neighboring blocks.

despair around the world. The news of a terrorist attack on U.S. soil spread over the airwaves. Once again, the immediacy of television and radio brought people across the nation to a vantage point just across the street from the incredible spectacle of destruction and determination. America and the world watched, live, as firemen, policemen, clergymen, housewives, anybody, everybody, struggled to find and free possible survivors.

In between broadcasts of the carnage, the government appeared before the cameras, reassuring the American people that they would see justice. President Bill Clinton vowed to capture the "evil cowards" responsible and Attorney General Janet Reno guaranteed that prosecutors would seek the death penalty. Special teams of federal investigators were deployed to find the killers.

Meanwhile, an Oklahoma Highway Patrol officer pulled over twenty-seven-year-old Timothy

Anybody, everybody struggled to find and free possible survivors.

McVeigh for a minor driving violation about ninety minutes after the bombing. The presence of weapons in his vehicle led to his being taken into custody. There was, of course, no suspicion at all that this Gulf War veteran could have had anything to do with the bombing; he was merely in violation of a traffic technicality.

There was little fear that this tragedy was homegrown. Radio and television broadcasters around the world were already speculating that foreign terrorists were responsible. The last U.S. terrorist attack—the bombing of New York City's World Trade Center in February 1993—had been organized by a foreign, militant Islamic group. America assumed similar forces were at work in Oklahoma. There were even reports that several possibly-Middle Eastern men were seen walking

Anticipation was high that a foreign terrorist group would soon claim the bombing as its handiwork.

away from the federal building. Anticipation was high that a foreign terrorist group would soon claim the bombing as its handiwork, with attendant pronouncements of their reasoning or possible demands. But no such announcement was made, and the grisly work of trying to free the buried people continued.

By April 21, several survivors had been pulled from the collapsed federal building, along with a mounting number of those who did not survive. That was also the day that authorities were scheduled to free McVeigh. But just before he was released from custody, was recognized as a suspect and charged with the bombing.

The broadcast news of McVeigh's arrest was a thunderous shock to the American system—all indications were that the worst terrorist attack in

Left to right:
Firemen sift through the rubble looking for survivors • A fireman carries Baylee Almon from the burning building that once housed the daycare center. Baylee was one of nineteen children who did not survive the explosion • Recovery workers used fire ladders and ropes to access the top floors of the building

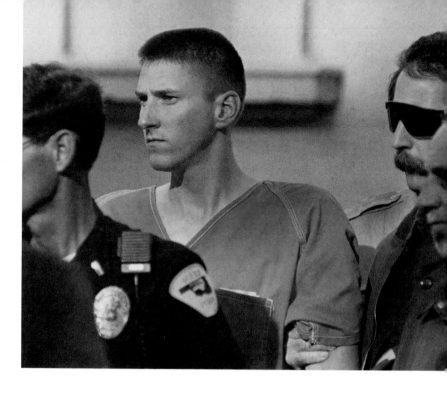

McVeigh's capture and subsequent sentencing could never answer the pressing question: "Why?"

Left to right:
Twenty-seven-year-old
Timothy McVeigh
is transported for
arraignment. He was
later sentenced to death
for his role in the
bombing • Mourners
placed flowers and stuffed
animals on the fence
surrounding the federal
building in memory of
the victims

the history of the United States was not the deed of some far-away crazed terrorists: this time, the horror came from within.

An acquaintance of McVeigh from the army, Michael Fortier, was taken into custody and supplied the information that led authorities to another McVeigh friend, Terry Nichols. Nichols voluntarily surrendered and was later charged in the bombing. Fortier pleaded guilty to a lesser charge and turned state's witness. He later received a twelve-year sentence.

Bodies continued to be pulled from the rubble for nearly two weeks. On May 4, 1995, the search for survivors ended. Hundreds of innocent people had been injured. The dead numbered 167, including nineteen children.

In addition to the massive memorial that took place just after the bombing, individual funerals dotted Oklahoma City's calendar in the weeks to come. For survivors and family members left behind, teams of therapists were made available. McVeigh's capture and subsequent sentencing would guarantee he would not cause such pain again, but it could never answer the pressing question: "Why?"

McVeigh's federal trial, held in Denver, Colorado, painted a right-wing extremist portrait of the defendant. Prosecutors believed it was no accident that Timothy McVeigh had visited David Koresh and the Branch Davidians and felt sure that the Oklahoma City bombing was related to anti-government feelings about what had happened outside Waco, Texas, exactly two years prior to the bombing.

In June 1997, the Denver jury convicted Timothy McVeigh of eleven counts of conspiracy and murder and condemned him to die by lethal injection. On December 23, 1997, a jury convicted Terry Nichols of conspiracy and eight counts of manslaughter. He was sentenced on June 4, 1998, to life imprisonment without the possibility of parole. Nichols was not subject to the death penalty because the jury did not reach a unanimous verdict on whether he was planning an attack "with the intent to kill."

In March 1999, Oklahoma prosecutors charged Nichols with state murder counts, vowing to try for the death penalty. At that time, McVeigh also faced state charges pending the outcome of an appeal of his federal conviction.

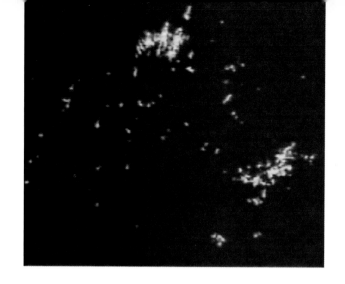

Flight 800
Explodes Over Atlantic

July 17
1996

Left to right: The flaming wreckage of Flight 800 floated in the water off Long Island for hours after the explosion • The U.S. Coast Guard and several local volunteers collected debris from the water

After the bombing of the World Trade Center in 1993 and the barbaric attack in Oklahoma City two years later, Americans were increasingly likely to suspect terrorism as a cause of major disasters on U.S. soil. Then, on July 17, 1996, just as the Atlanta Centennial Olympics were in full glory, a plane bound from New York to Paris met with tragedy.

On Wednesday, July 17, the Boeing TWA 747 that would become Flight 800 to Paris, had arrived in Athens, Greece, from New York's John F. Kennedy International Airport as Flight 880. The plane, now Flight 881, took off at 1:25 p.m., arriving in New York at 4:00 p.m. After routine maintenance, the plane, now Flight 800, rolled to the gate and began boarding its Paris-bound passengers.

Flight 800's passengers included people of all ages and walks of life—high-school students, honeymooners, artists, diplomats, and blue-collar

Passenger liners don't just explode in mid-air.

workers. They were going home, starting an adventure, pursuing an opportunity, making a routine business trip. Two hundred thirty people filed on board, saying their good-byes.

Just after 8:00 p.m., with doors secured and passengers buckled in, Flight 800 rolled back from the gate and taxied toward the runway. A few minutes later it was in the air, climbing eastward over Long Island on the way to Paris.

Thirty minutes after liftoff, Captain Steven Snyder raised the aircraft from thirteen thousand to fifteen thousand feet. His conversation with Boston Air Traffic Control and another crew member was preserved by the plane's flight data recorder. Such everyday words of flight lingo were the last heard from the plane.

Nearly eighteen minutes passed in uneventful silence. At 8:48 p.m., TWA Flight 800 exploded over the Atlantic Ocean, killing all on board.

Below:
A section of coach seats from Flight 800 are gathered from the ocean

Left to right:
Ninety-six percent of the plane was reconstructed for the benefit of FBI, FAA, and NTSB investigations • Vernon Ellingstad, NTSB Director of Research and Engineering, prepares to study the plane's flight data recorder

TWA's CEO Jeffery Erickson learned of the disaster while in London with other senior management. The executives were celebrating the company's one-year rise from Chapter 11 bankruptcy and vigorous fiscal recovery. News of the explosion of one of TWA's fifteen Boeing 747s brought their joy to an abrupt end.

Many Americans were watching the Olympics when the broadcast was interrupted by bulletins announcing the crash. Theories flickered across the news of possible terrorism, spurred on by the presence of the Olympics in Atlanta and the belief that passenger liners don't just explode in mid-air.

A massive sea and air rescue effort was mobilized, involving more than four hundred Coast Guard personnel and hundreds of volunteers in private boats. But other than wreckage, bodies, and luggage, the search and rescue teams only found remnants from the makeshift memorial mourners had crafted at the water's edge. In addition to searching for bodies and the flight data recorder, every piece of the plane that could be found was pulled out

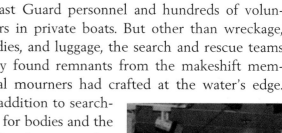

*They were going home,
starting an adventure,
pursuing an opportunity,
making a routine business trip.*

of the sea and carefully assembled in a hangar in Calverton, Long Island.

For the next sixteen months, the FBI, the Federal Aviation Administration, and the National Transportation Safety Board conducted an unprecedented investigation. Agents and scientists examined more than 96 percent of the plane

and explored every theory, from a bomb planted onboard to an errant U.S. missile strike.

The FBI ruled out all theories except the possibility of mechanical failure. Investigators ultimately concluded a spark of unknown origin ignited the vapors in the central fuel tank. The NTSB continues to investigate.

Above:
The beaches closest to the accident site became memorials for mourners

Atlanta Olympics *Bombing*

July 27
1996

Above:
Centennial Park was designed to let everyone enjoy the spirit of the Olympic Games without the need of tickets or oppressive security measures. Thousands crammed the area for special events and concerts

The annals of Olympic history are filled with vivid moments of glorious triumphs and devastating defeats that are engraved clearly and permanently in the collective memory. But there are also moments that, against the backdrop of the Games, appear to be nothing more than ugly images of cowardice. One such image that haunts the memory of an otherwise picture-perfect Olympics occurred in July 1996 during the Centennial Olympic Games in Atlanta.

Amid the tightest, most technologically advanced security in Olympic history, Centennial Park in downtown Atlanta was refreshingly accessible. Organizers had structured the park as a reprieve from sometimes oppressive security measures. With a sound stage, several corporate pavilions, and various other planned celebrations, Centennial Park was open to the general public—allowing tourists and athletes a chance to mingle freely.

Olympic revelers filled Centennial Park on the early morning of Saturday, July 27. Thousands were packed near the stage at the AT&T Global Olympic Village pavilion to dance to music provided by Jack Mack and the Heart Attack.

Atlanta's 911 bureau received an anonymous telephone call that was eventually traced to a pay telephone a mere three blocks from Olympic Village at 12:58 a.m. eastern time. The caller threatened, "There is a bomb in Centennial Park. You have thirty minutes." Shortly before the call, a security guard noticed an unattended green backpack near the sound tower. He alerted police. Once the bomb threat was phoned in, police called a team of bomb experts to the scene. Unsuccessful attempts then were made to clear the thousands of people from the park.

At 1:25 a.m., the bomb exploded, sending a combination of nails and shrapnel through the crowd in every direction. Centennial Park became

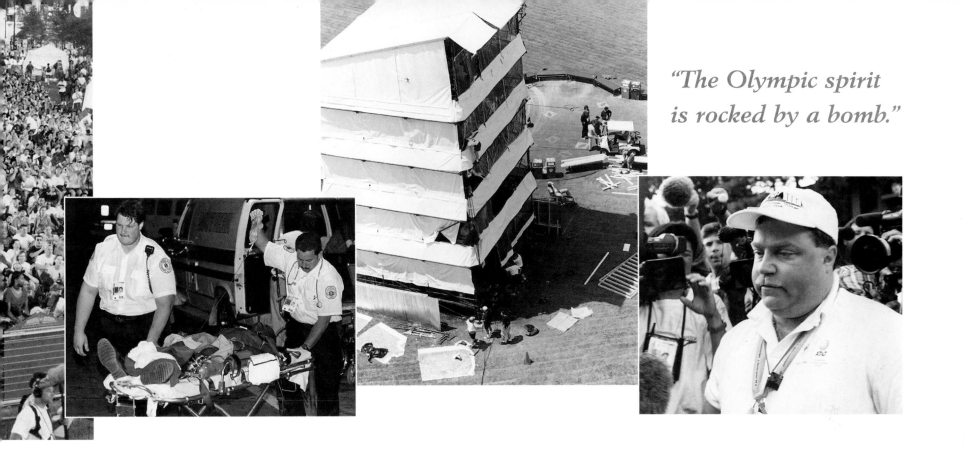

bedlam as thousands of people stampeded to the exits. Police sealed off the area, leaving access only for emergency vehicles to remove the victims. National Guard troops arrived to establish order and to find those responsible for the violence. In all, two were killed and 111 wounded.

The throng of global media already assembled in Atlanta began flashing bulletins of the apparent terrorist act to their audiences around the world. Analysts immediately made comparisons to the tragedy that had befallen the Israeli team twenty-four years earlier at the 1972 Munich Olympics. But soon the focus of the investigation would shift from the possibility of international terrorism to thirty-three-year-old Richard Jewell, the security guard who first spotted the suspicious knapsack.

Initially praised as a hero for his discovery, Jewell eventually fell under the watchful eye of investigators. Authorities wondered if he may have planted the bomb in order to "find" it and gain notoriety. FBI and ATF agents descended on

Jewell's apartment and ripped apart his personal history. Jewell's status as the focus of the investigation leaked to the press, and he moved to the center ring of a media circus for the next eighty-eight days.

Though never officially charged, the media tried and convicted Jewell on a nightly basis. He maintained his innocence throughout the ordeal, with family members televising tearful appeals on his behalf.

Ultimately, the investigation would turn up nothing that pointed to Jewell, and he was formally cleared by the investigative agencies on October 26. To date, the Centennial Park bombing remains an unsolved mystery.

Atlanta's experiment with giving everyone the opportunity of a relaxed Olympic experience had failed. Now, in the days after the bombing, there was an overwhelming need for increased security. The resulting tension not only affected Centennial Park's once-jubilant atmosphere, but that of the Games as a whole.

Left to right:
A victim of the bombing is transported to a nearby hospital. In all, two people were killed and 111 injured • Workers repair Centennial Park's television structure, the site of the explosion • Though the media tried and convicted former security guard Richard Jewell of the bombing, he was officially cleared by investigative agencies on October 26, 1996

Princess Diana
Dies

August 31
1997

Clockwise from bottom:
Diana, Princess of Wales •
Diana and Dodi Fayed
cruise off the coast of
Saint Tropez, France,
nine days before the
accident • The remains
of the Mercedes Benz
after crashing in a
central Paris tunnel

At nineteen, Diana Spencer was a pleasant, attractive young woman, a kindergarten teacher and nanny with a shy, retiring manner. The courtship between Diana and Charles Philip Arthur George, the Prince of Wales, was hailed as a fairy tale come to life and their marriage on July 29, 1981, was broadcast to a global audience numbering nearly one billion. The fairy tale continued as the Princess gave birth to Prince William in 1982 and two years later to Prince Harry.

Shortly thereafter, signs that all was not well with the Prince and Princess of Wales began surfacing in public. More and more, the couple began to lead separate lives. In December 1992, the couple separated, but it would be another four years before their divorce would be finalized.

While Diana no longer had official royal duties, her life was nonetheless the subject of relentless media curiosity. Diana made good use of this media attention to publicize the causes she

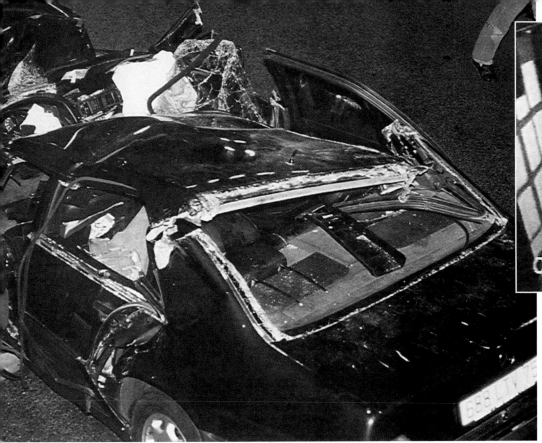

"Reports from Paris say that Princess Diana has died in a car accident that also killed her companion."

championed. Her presence brought publicity, as well as money, to organizations such as the United Cerebral Palsy Foundation and the British Red Cross' campaign against land mines. However, Diana brought more than this to her work, she also brought a tremendous humanity. Diana shook hands with AIDS patients and lepers. She held babies with HIV, visited terminally ill children, and walked through land-mine infested territory in war-torn Bosnia.

In the summer of 1997, Princess Diana was romantically involved with Dodi Fayed, the son of the wealthy Egyptian businessman, Mohammed Al Fayed, who was best known as the owner of Harrods, a venerable British department store. Dodi Fayed and Diana flew to Paris on the afternoon of August 30 and checked into the Fayed family-owned Ritz Hotel. At approximately 6:30 p.m., Dodi went to a Paris boutique to pick up the $200,000 diamond and emerald ring he and Diana had selected eight days earlier in Monaco.

At around 7:00 p.m. the couple drove from the Ritz to Dodi's apartment. Photographers were waiting for them. After a two-hour stay, the couple returned to the Ritz for a late dinner. By this time, the throng of photographers was so large that the couple had difficulty opening the car door. They began dinner in the Ritz restaurant, but the constant attention of other guests made Diana uncomfortable and they finished the meal in their room.

There were now thirty or so photographers waiting outside the hotel. At 11:15 p.m. a decoy car left from the front of the hotel while Princess Diana, Dodi Fayed, and Trevor Rees-Jones, their bodyguard, left from the rear in a Mercedes S-280 driven by Henri Paul, the acting head of security at the Ritz. The scheme was not completely successful and at least six photographers caught up with the couple by the time they reached the stoplight in the Place de la Concorde. Henri Paul headed onto the river-front expressway and accelerated to

Top to bottom:
Video footage from the Ritz Hotel shows Diana and Dodi Fayed (far right) speaking with driver Henri Paul moments before leaving • Princess Diana had struggled with the paparazzi since she came into the limelight. To many, the aggressive actions of the press share the blame for her death

speeds as fast as one hundred miles per hour as he entered the Alma tunnel. Approximately thirty seconds later, Paul lost control of the car and crashed into the tunnel's thirteenth pillar. The Mercedes came to rest against the wall of the tunnel with its horn blaring. Henri Paul and Dodi Fayed were killed instantly. Princess Diana and Rees-Jones were still alive, but trapped inside the car's twisted metal.

When the ambulance arrived, Diana was carefully extracted from the demolished car and received forty-five minutes of treatment, before she was taken to a nearby hospital.

Around the world, regularly scheduled broadcasts were interrupted before the ambulance carrying Diana had reached the hospital. Details surrounding the tragedy poured out of Paris through the night. The BBC and SKYTV in Europe, as well as NBC and ABC and the three cable news networks in the U.S., broadcast extended coverage until 3:00 a.m. eastern standard time on Sunday.

At 4 a.m. local time on August 31, 1997, Diana was pronounced dead from what physicians described as "massive chest injuries and hemorrhaging, followed rapidly by cardiac arrest."

Below:
(from left to right) Prince William, Earl Spencer, Prince Harry, and Prince Charles follow Diana's coffin into Westminster Abbey, September 6, 1997

"This is an opportunity for [the royal family] to thank all of you who have brought flowers...and paid your respects in so many ways to a remarkable person."

Later that day, Buckingham Palace released the following statement: "Buckingham Palace has confirmed the death of Diana, Princess of Wales. The Queen and the Prince of Wales are deeply shocked and distressed by this terrible news. Other members of the Royal family are being informed. Details of the funeral arrangements have yet to be confirmed."

The funeral took place on Saturday, September 6, in London's Westminster Abbey. The coffin was taken in procession from St. James Palace to the funeral service at Westminster Abbey. Her sons, Prince William and Prince Harry, walked behind the coffin accompanied by their father, Prince Charles, as well as the Duke of Edinburgh and their uncle, the Earl of Spencer. Two thousand people gathered at Westminster Abbey for the

funeral service. At the close of the service, those assembled and the nation observed a minute of silence. Outside, the Union Jack flew at half-mast.

Public debate on how to attribute blame for Diana's death will likely continue for years. Searching for an explanation after the accident, some wondered whether the pursuing paparazzi had pushed too far, while others suspected poor response by medical teams on the scene. Two years after the accident, a French magistrate cleared the reporters of all charges, placing blame on the driver Henri Paul, whose blood-alcohol level far surpassed the legal limit. Even so, the ruling still could not bring closure to the void felt around the world at the loss of Diana, the people's princess who had touched millions with her kindness, generosity, and humanity.

Left to right: Mourners covered the entry to Kensington Palace with flowers the day after Diana's death • Prince William and Prince Harry, accompanied by their father, Prince Charles, receive flowers from the mourning crowd

The Impeachment of *President Clinton*

Despite countless rumors of corruption and adultery, the office of the president of the United States has only suffered the scar of impeachment once. Once, that is, before William Jefferson Clinton took office. But for all the lies, the confessions, and a raucous media frenzy, the nation's leader came out on top.

The investigation of President Bill Clinton began with allegations of improprieties surrounding everything from a failed Arkansas real-estate deal, named Whitewater, to marital infidelity. Congressional committees dug into the President's and First Lady Hillary's background. In January 1994, charges from the Whitewater accusations resulted in an official inquiry by an independent counsel, a lawyer with no conflict of interest given the authority to prosecute high-level officials. Attorney General Janet Reno appointed Kenneth Starr to this position soon after the investigation began. But Democrats considered Starr to be less

than non-partisan, as he had served as Republican President George Bush's solicitor general.

In January 1998, Starr began pursuing allegations of the President's alleged sexual misconduct. Four years earlier, Paula Jones, a former state government secretary, sued the President for sexual harassment she claimed to have endured from Clinton when he was still governor of Arkansas. Part of what she alleged was a pattern of sexual misconduct. Monica Lewinsky, a former White House intern who had been rumored to be having an affair with the President, had been called to corroborate Jones' assertion.

Although both Clinton and Lewinsky denied the accusations, a former co-worker of Lewinsky, Linda Tripp, presented Starr with secretly recorded conversations between herself and Lewinsky. In Tripp's tapes, the intern bragged about having an affair with the President and suggested that Clinton and his friend Vernon Jordan had urged

"I did not have sexual relations with that woman, Ms. Lewinsky."

her to deny the affair. She also mentioned to Tripp that Jordan helped her find a job after leaving the White House in 1997. Starr interpreted this as a bribe to convince Lewinsky to cover up her relationship with the President.

Rumors of the affair persisted, and on January 26, 1998, following a White House ceremony and with the First Lady at his side, the President bolstered his position. Pointing his finger defiantly at the press gathered in the room, Clinton stated emphatically, "I did not have sexual relations with that woman, Ms. Lewinsky. I never told anybody to lie, not a single time, never. These allegations are false and I need to go back to work for the American people."

For the next few months, the government appeared to be at a near standstill as the House Judiciary Committee and political pundits debated the President's integrity, the credibility of his testimony, and where the line should be drawn between a president's public and private life. While the legions of the President's supporters and detractors became clear-cut, the line between legitimate press and tabloid journalism began to blur as more salacious details of the affair seeped out of the investigator's office. The President and the people around him were deposed. When questioned, Clinton stood by his previous denial, but by August 1998, his position began to appear more tenuous. The FBI was conducting DNA testing on the most incriminating evidence of all, a blue dress worn by Lewinsky during one of her encounters with the President. The dress, which Tripp had urged Lewinsky to save "as is," was said to be stained with Clinton's semen.

The President's affair with Monica Lewinsky had become irrefutable. On August 17, following four hours and twelve minutes of no-holds-barred closed-circuit testimony before the grand jury, Clinton faced the nation in a nationally televised

Left to right:
Clinton denies his affair with Lewinsky in a White House press conference, January 26, 1998 • Linda Tripp • Lewinsky's stained dress served as proof of the affair • Clinton's personal secretary Betty Currie (center) moves through a crowd of reporters on her way to testify before the grand jury

02-01-99 13:48:55

Presented in excruciating detail were the specifics of the affair between the President and his intern.

Left to right:
Monica Lewinsky gives
her testimony for the
Senate impeachment trial
• Independent Counsel
Kenneth Starr holds
a copy of his report
while testifying
before the House
Judiciary Committee,
November 19, 1998

address. This time, however, he admitted that he did have relations with Lewinsky and that it had been wrong to do so.

The networks scrambled to cover the confession. CBS moved their planned live telecast of the Miss Teen USA pageant to the following night, opting to air it on a tape-delay instead. ABC placated *Monday Night Football* fans by temporarily moving the broadcast to their cable network. NBC incorporated the President's speech into an expanded version of their popular newsmagazine *Dateline*. Clinton's mea culpa, lasting just over

four minutes, was broadcast across the dial to an audience of nearly sixty-eight million people, and drew mixed reactions from the media. CBS White House correspondent Bob Schieffer called it "an extraordinary statement," while ABC's Sam Donaldson wryly declared, "He didn't come clean tonight with the country."

On September 9, Starr issued a full report to Congress. Presented in titillating and excruciating detail were the contents of Tripp's secret tapes, the specifics of the affair between the President and his intern, their late-night phone conversa-

"It was chilling, unexpectedly chilling to hear the words."

tions, and the findings of the genetic testing proving that the DNA on Lewinsky's dress was Clinton's. The 445-page document purportedly contained "substantial and credible information" that the President had "committed acts that may constitute grounds for an impeachment."

Despite these revelations, and its objection to Clinton's lack of morals, the American public liked the way he was running the country. By winter of 1998, his job approval ratings rebounded to over 60 percent. Political experts believed the result of an impeachment to be a foregone conclusion—there was no way publicly elected officials would convict a President with so high an approval rating. And they were right.

Following two months of testimony and debate, on December 19, 1998, the House voted on four articles of impeachment and passed two of them—Article I, accusing President Clinton of committing perjury when he testified to the grand jury; and Article III, accusing the President of witness-tampering and obstruction of justice. The process then moved to the Senate, and on February 12, 1999, after a five-week trial, the Senate voted. Chief Justice William Rehnquist

was summoned to preside over the Senate and every network and cable channel carried the vote, with the proceedings appearing in the corner of the screen.

Cokie Roberts of ABC News commented that, "It's not suspenseful, but it is dramatic." Sixty-seven votes would be needed to convict and remove President Clinton. On the perjury count, the votes fell forty-five in favor, fifty-five against. On the charge of obstruction of justice, the Senate was evenly split: fifty votes for, fifty against. For a second time that afternoon, Chief Justice Rehnquist pronounced the President "not guilty," and then it was over. "It was chilling, unexpectedly chilling, to hear the words," said Brian Williams of NBC News.

It had been 386 days since the Lewinsky scandal was first reported. Nearly $50 million in taxpayers' money had been spent, $4.4 million to investigate the Lewinsky matter alone. All the time and money spent, the months of debate and speculation, and the political posturing that ripped Congress in half by party lines could not bring down the President. The nation returned to "politics as usual."

Left to right: Following the impeachment vote, Clinton addresses his supporters from the White Hose Rose Garden with Vice President Al Gore and First Lady Hillary at his side, December 19, 1998 • The Senate impeachment trial, February 12, 1999

Tragedy at Columbine
High School

April 20
1999

Top to bottom:
Eric Harris • Dylan
Klebold • Harris (left) and
Klebold returned to the
school cafeteria after
killing ten students in
the library. The two
committed suicide
minutes later

It took authorities eleven months to separate the gruesome facts from fiction, but in the final investigative report, one fact remained. On April 20, 1999, two heavily armed and horribly disturbed teenagers, Eric Harris, 18, and Dylan Klebold, 17, walked into their Littleton, Colorado, high school and calmly, sometimes jubilantly, murdered twelve fellow students and a forty-seven-year-old science teacher. The massacre ended when the two, denying their victims or their families justice, committed suicide before they were forced to face their punishment.

Among the student body of Columbine High School, Klebold and Harris found many enemies. Like countless other kids who didn't fit in, the two loners were taunted as misfits. But unlike other outcasts who find saner ways of coping, Klebold and Harris forged a bond from their feelings of hatred, and for more than a year, the two plotted their maniacal revenge.

On the morning of April 20, the two sat in their cars in the parking lot of Columbine High School, strapped on their guns and ammunition, and donned long black Western-type duster coats to conceal their weapons. By 11:17 a.m., it was apparent they'd have to improvise from their original plan. Neither the diversionary bomb they'd planted two miles from the school to distract police, nor the two propane bombs they'd hidden in the shool's cafeteria, had exploded. So the pair simply walked toward the school, raised their weapons, and opened fire.

Before they reached the school entrance, Klebold and Harris fatally shot two students and wounded five others, including art teacher Patricia Nielsen. Despite her injury, and while the two killers terrorized students in the crowded cafeteria, Nielsen managed to make her way to the school library and place a 911 call. "I'm a teacher at Columbine High School and there is a student here with a gun," she said. The dispatcher reassured Nielsen that the police were on their way. Meanwhile, Harris and Klebold were headed to the library and Nielsen could hear them outside the door. "Oh God! Oh God! He's outside the library! Kids, just stay down!"

Harris and Klebold entered the library as the police dispatcher listened on the open line. One of the teens fired off six shots and then they both began to laugh as their victims cried out in terror.

Left to right:
SWAT team members escort students to safety. Not knowing the identity of the killers, police were forced to treat all escaping students as suspects • A student clings to her mother outside the school. Many parents had to wait in a nearby elementary school for word of their children

"Oh God! Oh God!
He's outside the library!
Kids, just stay down!"

Left to right:
Patrick Ireland, 17, was
shot twice in the head
before managing to escape
out a second-floor window
• SWAT team members
rescue Ireland from a
head-first fall • Shaken
students support one
another as they walk to a
nearby recovery site

"Don't worry," one of them said in a sadistically reassuring manner, "you're going to be dead in a few minutes." Then, the pair proceeded to randomly shoot anyone in their sights.

Klebold spotted seventeen-year-old Kasey Ruegsegger, said, "Peekaboo," and shot her. Reugsegger survived. Harris found Cassie Bernall huddled under a table. He aimed his gun at her and asked tauntingly if she believed in God. Cassie replied, "Yes, I believe in God." He asked her, "Why?" and murdered her before she could answer. Then the two demanded that all of the jocks stand up, announcing, "We're going to kill every single one of you."

Over the police scanner in the newsroom of the Denver radio station KOA, News Director Jerry Bell heard the police dispatcher's report of "a shooting, and possibly two people down in front of Columbine High School." Bell, along with KOA reporters Cheryl Preheim and Amani Ali immediately headed for the school. At approxi-

mately 11:40 a.m., radio and television stations throughout the Denver area interrupted programming with reports of the shooting. Shortly after noon, KOA replaced the regularly scheduled *Rush Limbaugh Show* with live, uninterrupted, on-the-scene reports and eyewitness accounts. By mid-afternoon, the siege at Columbine High School was being broadcast all over the world.

The rampage in the library ended with ten students dead. Harris and Klebold then left and walked downstairs to the cafeteria. Except for abandoned backpacks, and four students hiding under tables, the cafeteria was deserted. The killers, thirsty from their bloody task, drank from cups deserted on the lunch tables.

The school was now surrounded by SWAT teams, firemen, and paramedics—eventually eight hundred policemen were stationed outside the school. Because they were treating it as a hostage situation, not one of them had entered the school. Police had trouble pinpointing the gunfire due to

The massacre left fifteen dead, twenty-three wounded, and the town of Littleton permanently scarred.

the noise of the school's fire alarms and, compounding the difficulty, kids calling from inside the school on their cellular phones jammed emergency switchboards. Uncertain of how many students may be involved in the rampage, police systematically escorted students as they escaped from the building, insisting their hands remain on their heads until they could be frisked.

At around noon, the killers made their way back to the library. After firing a few rounds out the window at the police, Harris and Klebold raised their weapons to themselves. By 12:05 p.m., they were dead.

The police were still not sure just how many killers were involved. Students had told them about the Columbine outcasts nicknamed the "Trenchcoat Mafia," a group identified by their long black trench coats. Klebold and Harris were initially thought to be a part of the group, but that was an assumption that would later prove to be untrue. Finally, at around 12:30 p.m., police SWAT

teams cautiously entered the building to begin searching. But for wounded science teacher Dave Sanders, it was too late. Paramedics were unable to revive him and Sanders died at the scene. In all, the massacre left fifteen dead, twenty-three wounded, and the town of Littleton, Colorado, permanently scarred.

Littleton was not the first community to be traumatized by an incident of random school violence. School shootings in Jonesboro, Arkansas, and Springfield, Oregon, preceded the tragedy at Columbine by nearly a year, and a shooting at Heritage High School near Conyers, Georgia, just a month later proved Columbine would not be the last. But the murder spree of Dylan Klebold and Eric Harris placed Columbine in the American lexicon of discussions of senseless violence, teenage alienation, and gun control. More than anything, Klebold and Harris wanted to leave this life as something more than two anonymous outcasts—and they did. They left as murderers.

Left to right:
A girl displays signs of peace and support at the Columbine memorial service • Students pay their respects at a makeshift memorial • Two friends mourn at the funeral of seventeen-year-old Rachel Scott

John F. Kennedy Jr.
Dies

July 16
1999

On November 25, 1963, America watched as three-year-old John F. Kennedy Jr., hand to forehead in his tiny tailored coat, saluted the casket of the father he hardly knew. Three days earlier, President John F. Kennedy had been slain by an assassin's bullet. The nation mourned for the family it considered so near royalty, they called it "Camelot." The country adopted "John-John" as its own little prince and, with great expectations, watched him grow into manhood.

Despite his mother's vigilant efforts to shield her children from the prying paparazzi, John Jr.'s every move was regularly show-cased on the covers of upscale magazines and supermarket tabloids alike. His good looks and charm earned him the status of America's most

eligible bachelor, and, in 1988, the distinction of being *People* magazine's "Sexiest Man Alive." His much-publicized love interests included several famous women, including singer Madonna and actress Darryl Hannah. New York gossip pages referred to him simply as "The Hunk," while one of the many biographies written about him crowned him "Prince Charming."

After serving as assistant district attorney in Manhattan for six years, John Jr. left the law to start a monthly magazine called *George* (named after George Washington), a risky publish-ing venture that sought to make the world of politics entertaining. And, to a degree, the magazine succeeded.

Finally, in 1996 and at thirty-five years old, America's most eligible bachelor got

America adopted "John-John" as its own and, with great expectations, watched him grow into manhood.

married. His bride, thirty-year-old Carolyn Bessette, was a tall, willowy blonde who had met John at a New York charity event while she was a publicist for clothing designer Calvin Klein. Carolyn and John were wed on September 21 in an ultra-private ceremony on Cumberland Island, off the coast of Georgia. Though there had been speculation in the press for months that the two were secretly engaged, there had been no public announcement of the wedding.

On July 16, 1999, John and Carolyn were headed to the wedding of his cousin Rory Kennedy, which was to be held the next day on the Kennedy family property in Hyannis Port, Massachusetts. John, who had earned a pilot's license the year before, had decided to fly them there. With them was Carolyn's older sister, Lauren Bessette, a Wall Street investment banker. John had offered to fly Lauren to Martha's Vineyard, where she would be staying at a house

once owned by his mother. From there, he and Carolyn would continue on to the wedding in Hyannis Port.

There was little daylight left when the trio took off from Essex County Airport in Fairfield, New Jersey. John was piloting his recently purchased Piper Saratoga II HP—a high-performance, single-engine private plane. The impending darkness, the fact that much of the route was over water, and the mid-summer heat-wave haze hanging overhead would have made the flight a tricky one, even for a veteran pilot. Under those conditions, the horizon, which gives a pilot his visual bearings, often disappears, causing spatial disorientation. If the pilot is not adept at flying by the plane's instruments, there is a serious potential for disaster.

It was early on the morning of July 17, 1999, when friends awaiting the arrival of John Jr., Carolyn, and Lauren reported the plane long over-

Clockwise from bottom left:
Both President Kennedy and his son enjoyed the water • John Jr. explores the White House • Kennedy unveils the inaugural issue of *George* magazine, September 7, 1995 • Kennedy and wife Carolyn Bessette shine in the media spotlight

Clockwise from left: Kennedy did not start flying lessons until his mother, who worried about his daredevil attitude, died. He received his pilot's license in 1998 • The media surround the Kennedy compound in Hyannis Port • A map of the recovery operations • Recovery of the fuselage of Kennedy's ill-fated plane

due, prompting local aviation authorities and the U.S Coast Guard to begin search and rescue efforts. NBC News was the first to break the story of the missing plane on the morning of July 17, at approximately 8:10 a.m. eastern time, and the nation watched, once again stunned by a tragedy involving the Kennedy family. The NBC and ABC television networks moved their scheduled sports programming to their cable networks, CNBC and ESPN respectively, in order to provide daylong, uninterrupted coverage. On CBS, anchor Dan Rather, who had covered the assassination of President Kennedy in Dallas thirty-six years earlier, became emotional as he reminded viewers how "America adopted this boy." And, once again, the world's press descended upon the Kennedy family.

By day's end, no survivors had been found, and desperately hopeful vigils gave way to agoniz-ing reality. Due to the unendurable water temper-ature and the lack of any sign of survivors, the search teams had abandoned hopes of rescue and were now engaged in a recovery mission.

America watched as debris—a baggage tag belonging to Lauren Bessette, various personal items, and pieces of the private plane—washed ashore on Martha's Vineyard. The belief that the plane had indeed gone down became real, but investigators could only look to local radar reports to find out exactly what had happened.

FAA reports state that a local radar installa-tion picked up the plane at twenty-two hundred feet, and just twelve seconds later, at thirteen hun-dred feet. The plane was hurtling toward thewater at speeds reported as high as seventy-five to one hundred feet per second, rendering the plane uncontrollable. All three passengers died upon impact with the cold Atlantic waters.

SANIBEL

Once again, the world's press descended upon the Kennedy family.

On Wednesday, July 21, the bodies of JFK Jr., his wife Carolyn, and his sister-in-law Lauren were recovered from the ocean floor seven miles off of Martha's Vineyard. The next day, their ashes were scattered in the ocean off the island's coast, following a private family service.

At JFK Jr.'s memorial service, which was held at the Church of St. Thomas More in Manhattan on Friday, July 23, his uncle, Senator Edward Kennedy, spoke for and to the nation in his eulogy: "We thank the millions who have rained blossoms down on John's memory. He and his bride have gone to be with his mother and father, where there will never be an end to love....We who have loved him from the day he was born, and watched the remarkable man he became, now bid him farewell." And with that, America's little prince was laid to rest.

Left to right:
The couples' ashes were scattered off the coast of Martha's Vineyard • Family members return from the burial at sea • Carolyn Kennedy Schlossberg and her daughter, Tatiana • Crowds of admirers lay tributes outside the couples' TriBeCa apartment

Acknowledgments

I want to express special thanks to the following people, without whom, this book may never have existed.

There simply are not the words to adequately express my admiration and appreciation of Dominique Raccah, President of Sourcebooks. She is a true visionary who was willing to take a risk and I will be forever indebted to her for this experience.

Thank you to the entire staff of Sourcebooks for your collective efforts and determination in making this book the best it could be.

I am extremely grateful to Todd Stocke, Managing Editor of Sourcebooks, for his dedication, his talent, his immeasurable patience, his unwavering perseverance, and his skillful diplomacy.

I would like to thank Rebecca Pasko, Production Manager, for her unalterably positive disposition, enthusiasm, and her gifts for transforming this vision into reality.

My thanks to Jennifer Fusco, Associate Editor of Sourcebooks, for editing, writing, and organizational talents second to none, and to Katie Funk and Amy Reagan, interns extraordinaire, for excelling at the difficult task of ensuring historical accuracy. Also to Raymond Bennett for his remarkably thoughtful writing and editing skills.

Thanks to Kirsten Hansen, whose visual talents and artistic skill created the stunning page spreads for each event.

I would like to express my deepest gratitude to Bill Kurtis for giving *We Interrupt This Broadcast* the most eloquent, profound, and compelling voice possible.

And to Mr. Walter Cronkite, the dean of broadcast journalists, there is unquestionably no greater honor for me as the author, than to have your Foreword at the beginning of this book. Thank you for your generosity.

I would like to express my sincerest gratitude to Mark Rowland for his incredible writing talents. I want to thank Marc Firestone, for his friendship, encouragement, counsel, and for directing me to just the right publisher. I would also like to thank Jeri Porter, assistant to Bill Kurtis, for her skillful coordination that kept us on schedule, and to Joan Dry at Kurtis Productions for coordinating publicity efforts. I want to thank Marlene Adler and Tara Mattson, from Mr. Cronkite's office, for their invaluable assistance in coordinating the Foreword, which is the icing on this cake. I am also grateful to Michael Shulman and Eric Rachlis at Archive Photo for their patience and expertise. Thank you to Dan Hill and Susanella Rogers for their writing contributions, and to Dan Kavanaugh, Jeff Lamont, and Pat Strafford for their support and encouragement throughout. Thank you to Lee Larson, Vice President and General Manager, and Jerry Bell, News Director, of KOA Radio in Denver for their tremendous cooperation.

Audio and
Announcer Credits

Audio Credits

Narration written by Mark Rowland, writer/producer of television documentaries
Research services provided by Michael Dolan
Bill Kurtis was recorded by David Huizenga, Kurtis Productions, Ltd.
Production and engineering by Dave Kephart at KSR, and Chris Lindsley

Archival audio provided by and copyright of:
ABC Sports, Inc.
Cable News Network, Inc.
CBS News Archives
KOA Radio, Denver, Colo.
NBC News Archives
Westwood One, Inc.

© ℗ 1998, 2000 Sourcebooks, Inc. All rights reserved. Unauthorized copying, reproduction, public performance, and broadcasting strictly prohibited. Any broadcast or transmission of any kind, in whole or in part, of the audio material contained on these compact discs is strictly prohibited without prior written permission of the publisher and the individual copyright holders. Manufactured in the United States.

Announcer Credits

The author and publisher would like to especially thank the broadcast journalists listed below, as well as those we were unable to identify, for their professionalism and compassion in keeping us informed during these events.

Herb Morrison	Jim McKay	Gary McKenzie	Jim Bohannon
Fulton Lewis Jr.	Steve Porter	Steve Powers	Bob Fuss
Walter Cronkite	Russ Ward	Ed Gello	Sean Hall
Ike Pappas	Mike Moss	Joe Ewald	Jerry Bell
Bob Jett	Robert Weiner	Bob Morrison	Kathy Walker
Bob Carrol	John Meyer	Howard Cosell	Al Verley
Don Hickman	Larry Backus	Joe Walsh	Dan Rather
Lou Wood	Dan Sears	Bob Brill	Scott Pelley
John Preston Smith	Duff Thomas	Jeff Finch	Byron Pitts

Photography Credits

All credits are listed by page number, in the order indicated on the pages.

Every effort has been made to correctly attribute all the materials reproduced in this book. If any errors have been made, we will be happy to correct them in future editions.

The Hindenburg Explodes *2* Archive Photos; *3* Archive Photos; Archive Photos; *4* Archive Photos; Archive Photos; *5* Archive Photos **Pearl Harbor Under Attack** *6* Archive Photos; *7* Archive Photos; *8* Archive Photos; *9* Archive Photos; Scott Swanson/Archive Photos **D-Day: The Normandy Invasion** *10* Popperfoto/Archive Photos; Express Newspapers/H 962/ Archive Photos; *11* Archive Photos; Archive Photos; *12* Popperfoto/ Archive Photos; Archive Photos; *13* Popperfoto/Archive Photos **President Roosevelt Dies** *14* Popperfoto/Archive Photos; *15* Archive Photos; Little White House State Historic Site; *16* Archive Photos/American Stock; Archive Photos/Morton Tadder; *17* Archive Photos **V-E Day: War in Europe Ends** *18* Archive Photos; *19* Archive Photos; Archive Photos/Yevgeny Khaldei; *20* Archive Photos; Archive Photos; *21* Archive Photos **Atomic Bomb Destroys Hiroshima** *22* Archive Photos; *23* Archive Photos; Archive Photos; Archive Photos; *24* Archive Photos; Archive Photos; *25* Archive Photos **Japan Surrenders: WWII Ends** *26* Archive Photos; *27* Archive Photos; Archive Photos; *29* Archive Photos; Archive Photos **Truman Defeats Dewey** *30* Archive Photos/Blank Archives; *31* Archive Photos; Archive Photos **General MacArthur Fired** *32* Popperfoto/Archive Photos **Sputnik Launched by Soviets** *34* Archive Photos; *35* Archive Photos/Nordisk Pressfoto; Archive Photos/Earl Young **John Glenn Orbits Earth** *36* Archive Photos; Archive Photos; *37* Archive Photos/Paris Match; *38* Archive Photos; *39* Archive Photos **Marilyn Monroe Dies** *40* Archive Photos/Frank Driggs; *41* Everett Collection; Archive Photos; *42* Archive Photos; Archive Photos; *43* Fotos International/Archive Photos **Cuban Missile Crisis: Nuclear War Threatened** *44* Archive Photos; *45* Archive Photos; *46* Archive Photos; *47* Archive Photos; Archive Photos; Archive Photos **President Kennedy Assassinated** *48* Archive Photos; Archive Photos; *49* Archive Photos; *50* Archive Photos; *51* Popperfoto/Archive Photos; CBS Photo Archive; Archive Photos/Consolidated News; *52* Archive Photos; *53* AP/Wide World Photos **Lee Harvey Oswald Assassinated** *54* Popperfoto/ Archive Photos; *55* Archive Photos; Archive Photos; *56* Popperfoto/Archive Photos; Popperfoto/Archive Photos; *57* Deutsche Press/Archive Photos **President Johnson Declines Re-election Bid** *58* Archive Photos; Archive Photos/Popperfoto; Archive Photos; *59* Archive Photos; Don Hogan Charles/New York Times Co./Archive Photos; *58* Archive Photos **Martin Luther King Jr. Assassinated** *60* Archive Photos; *61* Archive Photos; *62* Archive Photos; UPI/Corbis-Bettmann; *63* Archive Photos/A.F.P. **Robert Kennedy Assassinated** *64* American Stock/Archive Photos; *65* Archive Photos; Popperfoto/Archive Photos; *66* Express Newspapers/Archive Photos; Popperfoto/Archive Photos; *67* Archive Photos/APA; Agence France Presse/Archive Photos **Apollo 11: Man Walks on Moon** *68* Archive Photos; *69* Archive Photos; Archive Photos; *70* Archive Photos; Archive Photos; *71* Archive Photos; Archive Photos; CBS Photo Archive **Apollo 13: Astronauts Escape Disaster** *72* Archive Photos; *73* Archive Photos; *74* Archive Photos; Archive Photos; *75* Archive Photos **Kent State Massacre** *76* John Filo/Archive Photos; *77* Everett Collection; Everett Collection; *78* Everett Collection; Everett Collection; *79* Mike Lien/New York Times Co./Archive Photos; Archive Photos **Munich Olympics Tragedy** *80* Everett Collection/Cleveland State University Archives; *81* Express Newspapers/Archive Photos; Kurt Strumpf/AP/Wide World Photos; Deutsche Presse Agentur/Archive Photos; *82* UPI/Corbis-Bettmann; AP/Wide World Photos; *83* Archive Photos; Archive Photos; Deutsche Press Agentur/Archive Photos **Nixon Resigns** *84* Archive Photos; *85* Russell Reif/Archive Photos; Archive Photos; *86* Archive Photos; Archive Photos/Jim Wells; *87* George Tames/New York Times Co./Archive Photos; Archive Photos **Saigon Falls** *88* Agence France Presse/Archive Photos; Archive Photos; *89* AP/Wide World Photos; UPI/Corbis-Bettmann; *90* UPI/Corbis-Bettmann; *91* UPI/Corbis-Bettmann; UPI/Corbis-Bettmann **Elvis Dies** *92* Archive Photos; *93* © Elvis Presley Enterprises, Inc.; Archive Photos; Archive Photos; *94* Blank Archives/ Archive Photos; AP/Wide World Photos; *95* AP/Wide World Photos; Kirsten Hansen **Iran Hostage Crisis** *96* AP/Wide World Photos; *97* AP/Wide World Photos; AP/Wide World Photos; *98* AP/Wide World Photos; *99* AP/Wide World Photos; Archive Photos/Archive France **John Lennon Assassinated** *100* Archive Photos; *101* Archive Photos; AP/Wide World Photos/Alex Brandon; *102* Archive Photos; Mark Sherman/Archive Photos; *103* Reuters/Matt Slothower/Archive Photos **President Reagan Shot** *104* Archive Photos; *105* Archive Photos; Archive Photos; *104* AP/Wide World Photos **The Challenger Explodes** *106* Reuters/Archive Photos; *107* Reuters/Archive Photos; Archive Photos; *108* Archive Photos; *109* AP/Wide World Photos/ Jim Cole **Berlin Wall Crumbles** *110* Deutsche Presse/Archive Photos; Archive Photos; *111* Express Newspapers/Archive Photos; Express Newspapers/K708/Archive Photos; *112* Reuters/David Brauchli/Archive Photos; Reuters/David Brauchli/Archive Photos; *113* AP/Wide World Photos/Lionel Cironneau; AP/Wide World Photos/Thomas Kianzla; *114* AP/Wide World Photos/John Gaps; AP/Wide World Photos/Claus Eckert; *115* Reuters/Archive Photos **Operation Desert Storm Begins** *116* Reuters/Ina/Archive Photos; Reuters/Jonathon Bainbridge/Archive Photos; *117* AP/Wide World Photos; Cable News Network, Inc.; *118* Reuters/Charles Platiau/Archive Photos; *119* AP/Wide World Photos; Reuters/Caesar Assi/Archive Photos; *120* Reuters/Pat Benic/Archive Photos; Reuters/Russel Boyce/Archive Photos; *121* Reuters/Santiago Lyon/Archive Photos **Rodney King Verdict Incites Riots** *122* Reuters/Sam Mircovich/Archive Photos; AP/Wide World Photos; *123* Reuters/Lee Celano/Archive Photos; Reuters/Sam Mircovich/Archive Photos; *124* © 1992 Bob Tur/Robert Clark/LANS; © 1992 Bob Tur/Robert Clark/LANS; *125* Reuters/Lee Celano/Archive Photos **Waco Standoff Ends in Disaster** *126* Reuters/Ho/Archive Photos; *127* AP Wide World Photos; Reuters/G. Reed Schulman/Archive Photos; *128* Reuters/Reed Schulman/ Archive Photos; *129* Reuters/Calvin Hom/Archive Photos; AP/Wide World Photos **O.J. Simpson Saga** *130* Archive Photos/Darlene Hammond; *131* Reuters/Sam Mircovich/Archive Photos; Reuters/Sam Mircovich/Archive Photos; Reuters/Archive Photos; *132* Reuters/Sam Mircovich/Archive Photos; Archive Photos/Fotos International; *133* Reuters/Blake Sell/ Archive Photos **Oklahoma City Bombing** *134* AP/Wide World Photos/ David Glass; *135* AP/Wide World Photos/James Finley; AP/Wide World Photos/David J. Phillip; *136* Reuters/John Kuntz/Archive Photos; Sygma Photo News/Charles H. Porter IV; *137* AP/Wide World Photos/David J. Phillip; Reuters/Jim Bourg/Archive Photos; *138* Reuters/ Jim Bourg/Archive Photos; *139* Reuters/Jeff Mitchell/Archive Photos **Flight 800 Explodes Over Atlantic** *140* Reuters/RTV/Archive Photos; Reuters/ Archive Photos; *141* Reuters/Jeff Christensen/Archive Photos; *142* AP/ Wide World Photos; Reuters/Mark Cardwell/Archive Photos; *143* Reuters/ Mark Cardwell/Archive Photos; AP/Wide World Photos **Atlanta Olympics Bombing** *144* Reuters/Erico Sugita/Archive Photos; *145* Reuters/Jeff Vinnick/Archive Photos; Reuters/Mark Baker/Archive Photos; Reuters/ John Kuntz/Archive Photos **Princess Diana Dies** *146* Express Newspapers/ Archive Photos; Reuters/Stringer/Archive Photos; *147* Reuters/Charles Platiau/Archive Photos; Reuters/Stringer/Archive Photos; Big Pictures/ Archive Photos; *148* Reuters/Paul Hackett/Archive Photos; *149* Reuters/ Michael Crabtree/Archive Photos; Express Newspapers/ Archive Photos **The Impeachment of President Clinton** *150* Sygma; *151* Associated Press AP; Associated Press OIC; Associated Press AP; *152* Corbis; Associated Press AP; *153* Associated Press AP; Associated Press/US SENATE **Tragedy at Columbine High School** *154* Corbis; Corbis; Corbis; *155* Sygma; Associated Press AP; *156* Corbis Sygma; Corbis Sygma; Associated Press AP; *157* Corbis; Corbis; Corbis **John F. Kennedy Jr. Dies** *158* Corbis; Corbis; *159* Corbis; Corbis; Corbis; *160* Corbis; Corbis; Associated Press AP; Corbis; *161* Corbis; Corbis; Corbis; Corbis

Joe Garner

Joe Garner is the *New York Times* bestselling author of *And The Crowd Goes Wild* and is a twenty-year veteran of the radio business, including eleven years as an executive with Westwood One. His expertise on the media's coverage of major events has been featured on *Larry King Live, Weekend Today,* CNN, CBS *Up-to-the-Minute,* and hundreds of radio programs nationwide. Both *We Interrupt This Broadcast* and *And The Crowd Goes Wild* were bestsellers in the *Wall Street Journal, Publishers Weekly,* and *USA Today.* He is president of Garner Creative Concepts, Inc., an entertainment production company in Los Angeles.

Bill Kurtis

Bill Kurtis has been earning the respect of viewers, colleagues, and competitors in television journalism for over thirty years. His career has touched every facet of the most influential medium in our lives. Millions of viewers now join him each weeknight as he presents hour-long, in-depth documentaries on the A&E Network. His earlier broadcast career was spent with CBS, as an anchorman at WBBM-TV in Chicago and correspondent and anchor for CBS News in Los Angeles and New York. Currently, his creative efforts are focused on Kurtis Productions, Ltd., and he has become one of the country's foremost producers of documentaries for television. Bill is executive producer of three award-winning, prime-time series for the A&E Network: the Peabody Award-winning science adventure series, *The New Explorers with Bill Kurtis,* and the highly acclaimed *Investigative Reports* and *American Justice.* His first book, *Bill Kurtis on Assignment,* features accounts of his international reporting accompanied by over one hundred of his photographs.